Thérèse of Lisieux

Saints by Our Side

Thérèse of Lisieux

By Susan Helen Wallace, FSP

Foreword by Donna-Marie Cooper O'Boyle

BOOKS & MEDIA
Boston

Library of Congress Cataloging-in-Publication Data

Wallace, Susan Helen, 1940-2013.
  Thérèse of Lisieux / Susan Helen Wallace, FSP ; foreword by Donna-Marie Cooper O'Boyle.
    pages cm
  ISBN 978-0-8198-7513-6 -- ISBN 0-8198-7513-9
  1. Thérèse, de Lisieux, Saint, 1873-1897. 2. Christian saints--France--Lisieux--Biography. I. Title.
BX4700.T4W29 2015
282.092--dc23
  [B]

                    2014016385

Published by Pauline Books & Media, 50 Saint Pauls Avenue, Boston, MA 02130–3491

Printed in the U.S.A.

www.pauline.org

Pauline Books & Media is the publishing house of the Daughters of St. Paul, an international congregation of women religious serving the Church with the communications media.

1 2 3 4 5 6 7 8 9   20 19 18 17 16 15

· · · · · · · · · · ·

Contents

. . . .

Foreword

Saint Thérèse of Lisieux left her earthly life at the young age of twenty four. We might tend to assume that a twenty-four-year-old couldn't possibly have had much worthwhile to offer the world before she closed her eyes on this life. Perhaps we might also imagine that she couldn't have accomplished much that could be considered noteworthy in her whisper of a life—just two dozen years.

Yet, our Church thinks otherwise, values her wisdom, and has even declared Saint Thérèse of Lisieux a doctor of the Church!

What can we learn from Saint Thérèse, the simple, young cloistered Carmelite nun? How can a young twenty-four-year-old help us to grow in holiness?

Saint Thérèse's life was a mix of joy and labor wrapped in the peace of Christ. The young Thérèse expressed, "My only desire is to do the will of Jesus always!"[1] But, just because Thérèse possessed lovely desires and prayers, was raised in a loving family, and later entered a holy convent does not mean that she was free of struggles or pain. She once clued us in by remarking, "Do not believe I am swimming in consolations . . ."[2] Thérèse worked hard and prayed persistently. She loved Jesus very much and wanted to please him no matter what was happening in her life. She learned to trust him completely, realizing that the difficulties and challenges she was called to undergo greatly aided her spiritual growth. She once wrote:

> I find that trials help very much in detaching us from this earth. They make us look higher than this world. Here below, nothing can satisfy us. We cannot enjoy a little rest except in being ready to do God's will.[3]

Another time she wrote, "[I]n suffering we can save souls."[4]

Knowing that the great saints have endured suffering and have discovered deep meaning in it indeed helps us modern-day pilgrims. Saint Thérèse's words and example have deeply impacted my own life. Because of her loving example I view sufferings and challenges in an entirely new light, and I pray that souls can be saved by God's grace and for the grace of patience and surrender to whatever it is that God is calling me to do.

Thérèse's heart was full of love. This young saint in the making had endeavored to do everything with love—*everything*! She showered love upon her fellow sisters (even a persnickety one!) and offered many prayers and sacrifices for the salvation of souls. She possessed a deep desire to travel the world so that she could be a missionary for God.

But Thérèse soon discovered an essential and profound lesson that dramatically changed her life and that she has passed down to all of us.

A major turning point for Sister Thérèse was when she reflected on her vocation. She began to think about the vocation of others—of apostles, martyrs, crusaders, priests, saints, missionaries, prophets, doctors, and more. Because Thérèse loved Jesus very much she prayed from the deepest recesses of her heart and asked him to allow her to preach the Gospel on all five continents. But as she prayed Sister Thérèse was keenly aware of being "little" and "powerless."

She decided to open her Bible and read the First Epistle to the Corinthians. As she read about all of the wide-ranging gifts given to a variety of people, Thérèse's heart instantly felt very peaceful and satisfied. In reading the words, she discovered and intensely realized that it was love alone that caused all of Christ's members to act. Love comprised all vocations—without love, apostles and prophets could not preach, martyrs could not die for their faith, and so on.

Thérèse was very deeply moved and cried out to Jesus with great emotion. Exuberantly she declared, "O Jesus, my Love . . . my vocation, at last I have found it . . . MY VOCATION IS LOVE! . . . [I]n the heart of the Church, my Mother, I shall be *Love*."[5]

Thérèse's life turned into an arresting testament of love. Nothing else but love mattered to Thérèse. Jesus' love sustained Thérèse through every suffering she was called to endure. She knew without a doubt that Christ's love was the remedy for everything.

Saint Thérèse's great love didn't stop when she left her earthy life. No, she deeply desired to labor even into eternity. She said, "I feel that my mission is about to begin, my mission of making others love God as I love Him. . . . If God answers my requests, my heaven will be spent on earth up until the end of the world."[6]

Saint Thérèse is an exemplary example for us to follow today. Her simple life of love and devotion can teach us that our obedience to our own state of life is essential to our journey toward heaven. Saint Thérèse fully surrendered her life to God. Though she wanted to become a missionary, she accepted her life of prayer and work in the convent, knowing in her heart that God had chosen it for her. By living this way, her humble and brief life made an enormous impact on our world.

We can indeed realize that our own lives can make a huge difference, too, when we surrender our hearts fully to God's will—as Saint Thérèse did—trusting him with the joys and sorrows and allowing him to love through us.

This book is an exceptional and tender look into the life of a simple saint whose love for Jesus and souls has dramatically changed the world. With every turn of the page, Saint Thérèse will become more alive in your heart, inspiring you to strive for holiness.

Like Saint Thérèse of Lisieux, let us, too, endeavor to live a life of love! Saint Thérèse of Lisieux, please pray for us!

DONNA-MARIE COOPER O'BOYLE

. . . .

Preface

Saints reflect the image of Jesus in their faces, and they bear the marks of his wounds on their souls. To imitate Christ in the time, location, and circumstance in which we find ourselves can easily seem beyond our reach.

How do you define the saints? As people who do great things? Oftentimes they are. But before they do great things for God, they love Jesus totally. Love transforms people into saints. God's love is infinite. It is the Holy Spirit alive in the Trinity of Father, Son, and Spirit. The love of the Father and the Son is the Holy Spirit. The Spirit's love in human beings is a transforming power. Only this love can transform people into saints. Love is the secret, the motivation. Through reflection and prayer, Saint Thérèse of the Child Jesus, a young Carmelite nun, found this secret: "Oh! How sweet is the way of Love! How I want to apply myself to doing the will of God always with the greatest self-surrender!"[1]

Thérèse was born in the Martin family home at 36 Saint Blaise Street, Alençon, France, on January 2, 1873. She died around 7:20 P.M., on Thursday, September 30, 1897, at the Carmel in Lisieux, France. She was not quite twenty-five. She lived almost a quarter of a century and was buried on October 4, 1897, in a quiet town cemetery in Lisieux. And that should have been all there was to it.

Of course, the Carmelite prioress would write about Sister Thérèse for their archives, and Masses would be said for the repose of her soul. But we may ask ourselves: What happened to spread this young woman's fame around the world? What is the story behind the nun and the power behind the story?

This is a biography of Thérèse of the Child Jesus and the Holy Face, also known as the "Little Flower." As we read her story and hear her own interpretation of the power of God in her life, we will be challenged to find a message for ourselves. Thérèse will demonstrate what can happen when people give themselves over to God. Thérèse's God is the loving Father who picks her up when she cannot climb the steep hill of perfection. Thérèse's God is the Crucified One whose scarred hands reach out to embrace her. Thérèse's God is infinite love, the Holy Spirit who fills her soul with himself. Her story is more than a biography. It is a divine takeover, a magnificent conquest on the part of God.

Thérèse invites us to let God do for us what he did for her. She will manifest to us the truth of Scripture: "God is love" (1 Jn 4:8). This book is offered as an introduction to Saint Thérèse and includes excerpts from her own writings and conversations. Quotations are taken from her autobiography *Story of a Soul* (which she was asked to write by her superiors), *Last Conversations,* and *The Poetry of Saint Thérèse of Lisieux*. Saint Thérèse has a word for everyone who comes in contact with her. Above all, she wants to bring us to her loving God. She wants to teach us how to love and let ourselves be loved.

CHAPTER ONE

• • • • • • • • • • •

Beginnings

Thursday, January 2, 1873 was cold and the sky a steel gray in Alençon, France. As night set in, the Martin family kept their vigil. Zelie's baby was born at 11:30 P.M. The family clustered around the big double bed, their eyes riveted on the infant in Zelie Martin's arms. Louis Martin leaned over and lightly stroked Zelie's hair. Her face was lined and tired-looking, but she was peaceful. Louis would be fifty years old that August; Zelie was forty-one. The little girl in her arms was to be their ninth and last child. Five of the Martin children lived. Three had died as infants; one, Helene, had died at the age of five.

Louis and Zelie decided on what to name the baby: Marie Françoise Thérèse Martin. And the family would call her Little Thérèse.

Marie, Pauline, Léonie, and Céline looked on and tried to be helpful. Their sister was robust, they thought, probably nearly eight pounds. But Mama had more experience and she guessed six pounds. Marie would be thirteen on February 22; Pauline would be twelve on September 7; Léonie, ten on June 3; and Céline, four on April 28. In between Léonie and Céline, Helene, Joseph-Louis, and Joseph-Jean-Baptiste had been born but had not survived. Between Céline and Thérèse had come Melanie-Thérèse, who had also gone home to God.

Louis lifted the tiny child and secured the soft blanket around her. Thérèse rested easily against his chest, over his heart. She slept peacefully unaware of the admiring glances and the bonds of love that surrounded her. Louis Martin walked slowly, quietly around the room, rocking the baby. He was experienced at this, and the girls watched with admiration. Zelie Martin dozed off while Thérèse's sisters waited for their father to tire so that they could hold their new sister too.

Louis and Zelie Martin

Louis Martin had been born on August 22, 1823 at Bordeaux, France, and was from a military family. He was quiet, gentle, organized, and patient. He excelled at his watchmaking trade because of his diligence and patience. He excelled in business because of his integrity. When he was twenty-two and single, Louis considered a religious vocation. The life of a monk, honed by prayer, contemplation, and work, had appealed to him. Because he had no background in Latin, however, he was not accepted as a candidate for the monastery.

Alençon was a peaceful town, quiet for its population of 13,600. Despite its smallness, however, Louis Martin and Zelie

Guerin were not to meet for several years, nor marry until he was thirty-five and she twenty-seven. Both loved their Catholic faith and both felt at one time in their adult lives a call to follow a religious vocation. Each had been advised against it: Louis for lack of education; Zelie for lack of health.

Zelie's childhood had been lonely, as she once reminded her brother Isidore Guerin. Their mother had spoiled Isidore and treated Zelie harshly, something she lamented with sadness. Zelie and Isidore's sister Elise became a Visitation nun, Zelie a lace-maker, and Isidore a pharmacist.

The love and affection Zelie received from her sister and brother helped her to bear the stern treatment of her parents. When Zelie married Louis Martin in the Church of Notre-Dame on July 13, 1858, a joy she had never known unfolded for her. She and Louis had so much in common, and they were in love. For the first ten months they lived a celibate marriage by mutual consent. Then a priest helped them to reconsider, and the Martins began having children. The world can be grateful for the priest who successfully convinced the Martins to have their family. If he had not done so, we would have been deprived of Saint Thérèse of Lisieux. Zelie and Louis were warm and affectionate with each other and their children. Their home was joyful and their children were happy.

First Separation

Marie Françoise Thérèse was a beautiful addition to the Martin's loving family. She was baptized on Saturday, January 4, when she was two days old. The oldest Martin child, Marie, was the baby's godmother. A few weeks later the baby developed intestinal difficulties. That situation leveled off, but when Thérèse was three months old, sickness struck again. Zelie wrote: "She is very bad and I have no hope whatsoever of saving her. The poor little thing suffers horribly since yesterday. It breaks your heart to see her."[1] Zelie Martin realized that Thérèse needed nourishment and fresh country air. The family doctor recommended that Thérèse be given into the care of a wet nurse for as long as necessary. And so a woman named Rose Taille was found to care for Thérèse.

Rose Taille was a hardy, healthy woman who lived on a farm eight miles outside of Alençon, in the village of Semalle. Little Thérèse shared the life of the Taille family from March 15 or 16, 1873, to April 2, 1874. The little girl grew and put on weight. Her curly hair, bleached by the sun, lent a healthy glow to her tanned complexion. Thérèse loved the flowers and animals. Zelie Martin wrote: "Her nurse brings her out to the fields in a wheelbarrow, seated on top of a load of hay; she hardly ever cries. Little Rose says that one could hardly find a better child."[2]

When Thérèse returned home over a year later, the Martins welcomed her with joy and genuine excitement. Their baby was lively and playful. She was alert and her eyes sparkled with delight. She missed the Taille family for a while, but the Martins showered so much affection on their fifteen-month-old that Thérèse was soon as contented as she had been on Rose's farm.

Céline and Thérèse through Mama's Eyes

While Thérèse got used to life at home, Marie and Pauline attended the Visitation boarding school, living there while classes were in session. Zelie Martin's letters to her daughter, Pauline, give glimpses into the personality and temperament of her two youngest children. Thérèse quoted her mother's carefully preserved letters in her autobiography, *Story of a Soul.*

> In the story of my soul, up until my entrance into Carmel, I distinguish three separate periods. The first is not least fruitful in memories in spite of its short duration. It extends from the dawn of my reason until our dear mother's departure for Heaven.[3]

The girls were three and a half years apart, and Thérèse would call Céline "the little companion of my childhood." From the time Thérèse returned from the Taille family, she and Céline were inseparable. The fifteen-month-old Thérèse looked up to Céline, and the two would laugh and play together.

On May 14, 1876, Mama wrote to Pauline:

> My little Céline is drawn to the practice of virtue; it's part of her nature; she is candid and has a horror of evil. As for the little imp, one doesn't know how things will go, she is so small, so thoughtless! Her intelligence is superior to Céline's, but she's less gentle and has a stubborn streak in her that is almost invincible; when she says "no" nothing can make her give in.[4]

Zelie also noticed that Thérèse, though younger than Céline, insisted on having her own way. Zelie realized that Céline quickly gave in. In her December 5, 1875 letter to Pauline, Zelie wrote of Thérèse:

> I am obliged to correct this poor little baby who gets into frightful tantrums; when things don't go just right and according to her way of thinking, she rolls on the floor in desperation like one without any hope. There are times when

it gets too much for her and she literally chokes. She is a nervous child, but she is very good, very intelligent, and remembers everything.[5]

Marie returned from boarding school while Pauline remained away from home. Since Céline was older than Thérèse, she had daily home classes with Marie. Little Thérèse felt left out and would begin to cry. That was more than Marie could bear so, Thérèse came into the room too. She was given a comfortable chair and some busy work, such as cloth to sew or beads to thread. While Céline learned her lessons, her little sister would get her needle tangled up in thread and the tears would start again. "Marie consoles her very quickly, threads the needle, and the poor little angel smiles through her tears," Zelie wrote to Pauline.[6]

As the years passed, Thérèse's love for Céline grew. "I remember that I really wasn't able to be without Céline," Thérèse wrote. When Thérèse was still too young to go to church on Sunday, Zelie would go to another Mass and stay behind with Thérèse. The spirited little girl would wait eagerly for sounds of the family returning from Mass. Céline would often bring home blessed bread and the two children would have a prayer service made solemn with a Hail Mary and a Sign of the Cross. Once, Céline could not bring home blessed bread. "Then make some," Thérèse commanded. Céline got a loaf of bread out of the cupboard, cut off a piece, prayed over the bread, and then the two girls ate it.[7]

Zelie recorded one spiritual conversation of Thérèse and Céline. Céline asked Thérèse: "How is it that God can be present in a small host?" "That is not surprising, God is all powerful,"

Thérèse answered. "What does all powerful mean?" asked Céline. Thérèse's answer was prompt and sure: "It means He can do what He wants!"[8]

"I Choose All!"

Zelie Martin documented many stories about Thérèse that help us to understand her developing personality. On May 10, 1877, just before Thérèse's older sister Léonie's fourteenth birthday, she wrote to Pauline that Léonie realized she was growing up. She gathered up her childhood treasures—doll clothes, fancy materials, and her doll—and placed them in a basket. Céline and Thérèse eagerly eyed the basket as Léonie set it on the floor:

> "Here, my little sisters, choose," Léonie said. "I'm giving you all this." Thérèse wrote: Céline stretched out her hand and took a little ball of wool that pleased her. After a moment's reflection, I stretched out mine saying: "I choose all!" and I took the basket without further ceremony."[9]

Remembering the incident vividly as an adult religious, Thérèse was able to find in her reaction to that situation a response that would indicate how she would approach the whole of her life with God.

> I understood . . . there were many degrees of perfection and each soul was free to respond to the advances of our Lord to do little or much for Him, in a word, to choose among the sacrifices He was asking. Then, as in the days of my childhood, I cried out: "My God, I choose all!" I don't want to be a *saint by halves*, I'm not afraid to suffer for You, I fear only one thing: to keep my *own will*; so take it, for "I *choose all*" that You will![10]

Thérèse and Her Father

Thérèse's trusting relationship with God the Father can be connected with her father's loving presence throughout her life. Louis Martin turned fifty the year Thérèse was born. His hair was graying and thinning, making him look continually more distinguished. Céline and Thérèse could have been his grandchildren. He enjoyed them so much, especially Thérèse. She would listen for the sound of her father's key in the front door at the end of the day. When she heard the click—and she always did no matter where she was in the house—she came running, leading the welcome committee. She would call "Papa, Papa," and hug her delighted father. Then she would sit on his foot, pony-fashion, and ride her father's shoe into the sitting room.

Zelie, busy about the house, would ask her husband in a light-hearted way why he spoiled Thérèse. Louis, shrugging his shoulders sheepishly, would reply, "Well, what do you expect? She's the queen!"[11]

One time, however, Thérèse was in a different mood. She was having fun on the swing in the garden, swinging higher and higher and feeling very independent. Her father walked down the garden path. "Come and kiss me, little queen," he called gently. Thérèse's blond curls fluttered in the breeze as her swing kept pace with the rhythm in her ears. "Come and get it, Papa!" she called flippantly.[12] Louis was hurt and quietly refused, walking into the house. Marie, overhearing the incident, stopped her little sister's swing and helped her to understand that her behavior was not right. She had answered their father rudely and had hurt his feelings. The little girl was overcome with remorse. She began to cry loudly. Her sobs filled the big house and she climbed the steps without waiting for help. She found her father and flooded him with affection. The little queen was quickly forgiven.

One thing stands out about Thérèse's earliest years: she was much wanted, much loved. She wrote: "All my life God was pleased to surround me with love, and my first memories are imprinted with the most tender smiles and caresses!"[13]

CHAPTER TWO

A Time of Change

The first phase of young Thérèse's life was filled with joy and childhood fun. Only an infant when sickness had gripped her, the Martin family bore the worry and pain. Now at the age of four, Thérèse would experience a sorrow that she would never forget.

Doctors had discovered that Zelie Martin was suffering from cancer. At that time the cancerous tumor she had carried for several years was considered inoperable. As Zelie drew close to death, she looked pale and dwarfed in her big bed. Thérèse and Céline observed the tense faces of Papa, Marie, Pauline, and Léonie. The two youngest knew they shouldn't talk. They stayed near their father like little statues while the adults moved around them, taking care of their mother's needs. The priest administered the Anointing of the Sick while their father's silent tears turned into sobs. Thérèse stayed near her father and wanted to tell him not to cry. She wanted Jesus to make her mother well again, but she only became sicker. In the early morning hours of August 28, 1877, Zelie died. She was forty-six years old.

Thérèse could sense what death was because of her family's reaction. She experienced a new emotion: a feeling of aloneness. She stayed near her father and Céline, quiet and very alert. Her father would take care of things; he would know what to do. After a long time, the tears of the Martin family ceased. Thérèse distinctly remembered standing quietly near her father beside her mother's coffin. Louis lifted Thérèse gently and said to his four-year-old: "Come, kiss your poor little mother for the last time."[1]

The day of Zelie's funeral her children stood around silently. Louise Marais, who was the Martin's maid until Zelie's death, said to the girls: "Poor little things, you have no mother any more!"[2] Céline quickly asked Marie if she would be her mother. Thérèse usually copied Céline's example, especially because her sister was three-and-a-half-years older. Thérèse hugged Pauline and cried: "Well, as for me, it's Pauline who will be my Mama!"[3]

Les Buissonnets

Slowly the family returned to their day-to-day living. The two older girls took over many of the responsibilities of managing the house and raising the smaller children. Thérèse idolized Marie and Pauline who brought so much love into her life. She said of her father, who had suffered more than anyone over the loss of his wife: "Our Father's *very affectionate heart* seemed to be enriched now with a truly maternal life!"[4] Despite the continued loving affection, little Thérèse became pensive and cried easily.

Louis Martin felt the weight of the loss of his wife. He began toying with the idea of relocating his family to Lisieux, about sixty miles away from Alençon. Zelie's brother, Isidore Guerin, owned the local pharmacy there. He and his wife would be supportive and loving. Louis Martin esteemed Isidore as though the man were his own brother. The Guerin girls, Jeanne, nine, and Marie, seven, would be friends and schoolmates of the younger Martin girls.

On November 15, 1877, Louis Martin and his family boarded a horse-drawn carriage and said their good byes to Alençon. Marie and Pauline felt the move deeply. It was hard to leave the friends, neighbors, and favorite pastimes they had grown up with. The move, coming as it did so close to their mother's untimely death, was like another death. But Louis felt sure that his family would adjust quickly once they were settled in Lisieux. The carriage moved ahead. The driver reined the horses in front of the Guerin home. The Guerins were expecting them. Jeanne and Marie were at the door, eager to greet their relatives and bring them into their home to a hot meal and the warmth of the fire.

Thérèse was excited. Her eyes became bright and eager once again, as when her mother was alive. She later wrote: "I experienced no regret whatsoever at leaving Alençon; children are fond of change, and it was with pleasure that I came to Lisieux."[5]

The next morning Isidore Guerin escorted his relatives to their new home. It was located in a quiet neighborhood, next to a park. The house had an English garden in the front yard and a vegetable garden in the back. It was spacious and ornate. Thérèse liked it, especially the well-lit belvedere at the top of the house.

Louis Martin soon lined the walls of the belvedere with books, making it his study. On bright days the warmth of the sun's rays penetrated the gray and cold of winter. Thérèse would grow to love the belvedere, especially because it was her father's domain. There he was king and his youngest daughter agilely mounted the stairs at will for an audience with him.

The Martin's new home received its name—*Les Buissonnets* (The Little Bushes)—because of the small bushes that bordered the front yard.

Life at Les Buissonnets

There was something entrancing about *Les Buissonnets*. Lively four-year-old Thérèse loved the security of the large spacious rooms where she could romp and play games with Céline. During those early years, Thérèse began to take home lessons from Marie and Pauline. Marie taught her writing and Pauline taught her catechism, sacred history, and grammar. The youngest Martin liked her classes, especially catechism and sacred history, and she did well in those subjects. But grammar was another story. Thérèse wrote: "Grammar frequently caused me to shed many tears."[6] But Thérèse's overall academic performance reflected dedication and a maturity beyond her years. She would climb the stairs to the belvedere at lunchtime to report the results of the classes to her "king." Sometimes she had an award to show her father as she went over her grades with him. He would lift Thérèse onto his lap and hug her, calling her his little queen.

As the seasons changed and sunny days transformed the grounds of *Les Buissonnets* into a sea of flowers, grass, and a thriving vegetable garden, Thérèse loved to play outdoors. Her father would go out to the backyard with a book or paperwork to keep Thérèse and Céline company while they played. When Céline was at school with Léonie, Thérèse had her father all to herself. During the months when the weather was warm, father and daughter would take an afternoon walk. They would make a short pilgrimage to one of the nearby Catholic churches or a convent chapel to make their daily Eucharistic visit.

Thérèse continued to store up happy memories of life at *Les Buissonnets*, especially on Sundays and feast days. Going to church as family, sharing meals, taking walks, being part of conversations and games, visiting relatives, saying evening prayer together—all of this deepened her realization of how much she was loved. Thérèse sat next to her father at Mass. She looked up at him frequently, especially during the homily. She always listened intently to Father Ducellier, although she could not really understand the meaning of the homilies. The first homily she understood was on the passion of Jesus. It impressed her deeply, and she never forgot it.

One Sunday evening as Louis and Thérèse walked home from the Guerins' home, Thérèse looked up at the stars. The night was clear and the little girl noticed that one cluster of stars was shaped like a "T." "I pointed them out to Papa and told him my name was written in heaven."[7]

Thérèse also vividly recalled the first time she and her father prayed in the Carmelite chapel. He pointed to the grille, which looked like a strange wall of bars to Thérèse. Louis Martin explained that the nuns lived behind that grille. Thérèse wrote later: "I was far from thinking at that time that nine years later I would be in their midst!"[8] Father and daughter would walk home, hand in hand. Louis Martin usually bought Thérèse a treat, and then she would do her homework. When her daily assignment was completed, she would resume playing in the garden.

Thérèse loved to play tea party and mix her special brew of bark, seeds, and water. Her father was her privileged guest at every tea party. She offered her concoction to him, and he would pretend to be so pleased. Thérèse, of course, would pour some for herself as well. She and her father would chat politely and pretend to drink their tea. When the social was over, he would ask softly out of the corner of his mouth if he should throw out the liquid. Thérèse occasionally directed that the mixture be thrown away, but usually she kept it in the hopes that there would be another tea party later that day.

Lessons Not in Books

Thérèse was content to play in the little backyard patch that was her garden. But some days her father would also take her fishing. While Louis Martin fished, Thérèse would sit quietly nearby in the grass amidst the wild flowers. She would think deep thoughts, of which she would later write:

> Without knowing what it was to meditate, my soul was absorbed in real prayer. I listened to distant sounds, the murmuring of the wind, etc. At times, the indistinct notes of some military music reached me where I was, filling my heart with a sweet melancholy. Earth then seemed to be a place of exile and I could dream only of heaven.[9]

On one particular afternoon, when the sun's rays bathed Thérèse's face, she thought about God, her mother, and heaven. She watched her father fishing contentedly. She felt that Jesus was present in her whole being, that he knew her personally, that he loved her personally the way her father did—only more because God is God.

The afternoon passed quickly, and it was time to eat the treats that Thérèse had brought from home. Pauline had prepared the food while Thérèse watched with interest. Her sister had cut slices of freshly baked bread and coated them generously with jam. Sitting on the hillside now, Thérèse gazed down at the basket and remembered how the jam had glistened when the bread was first prepared. She hoped that her father was ready for his snack because she certainly was.

Louis put his fishing gear away and sat down next to Thérèse. They said a prayer and then Thérèse opened the basket. As an adult, she wrote of this incident to Pauline:

> The *beautiful* bread and jam you had prepared had changed its appearance: instead of the lovely colors it had earlier, I now saw only a light rosy tint, and the bread had become old and crumpled. Earth again seemed a sad place and I understood that in heaven alone joy will be without any clouds.[10]

On another afternoon, while her father fished, Thérèse enjoyed looking at all the wild flowers while thinking about the God who made them. Clouds suddenly rolled in and covered the sun like a shutter. It began to rain. Louis called for Thérèse to come along as he hastily packed his fishing gear. The raindrops grew bigger. Thunder rolled and lightning flashed. Louis wanted to take the shortest way home, which would take them through fields with grass taller than Thérèse. Louis lifted his daughter onto his back and picked up his rod and bait. Then he walked swiftly, cutting through several fields, until they arrived home. Although her father could hardly have agreed with her, Thérèse thought the adventure was thrilling.

When Thérèse was six, she and her father were distributing alms as they did on a regular basis. Louis realized that it is easy to admonish children to be grateful for what they have, to appreciate their blessings, and to share cheerfully with the less fortunate. But he never preached just with words. His quiet, continuous example was his sermon. His youngest child watched transfixed as her father listened to the needs of one person after another. He gave money, helped people find jobs, and made recommendations. Thérèse stayed close to him, hanging on every word.

As father and daughter were on one of their walks, an invalid on crutches dragged himself ahead. Thérèse felt his pain and frustration as he inched along the sidewalk. She slipped her hand out of her father's and ran up to the man, holding out her one coin to him. That was all the money she had at the moment and she just wanted to share the man's burden, to lighten his pain. But the man did not accept the coin. He shook his head and smiled sadly as he continued on his way.

The little girl's heart ached. Perhaps he would like the small cake her father had just bought her a short while before, but she didn't want to hurt her father's feelings either. Thérèse wanted to help the man, and she suddenly realized how she could do it.

I remembered having heard that on our First Communion Day we can obtain whatever we ask for, and this thought greatly consoled me. Although I was only six years old at this time, I said: "I'll pray for this poor man the day of my First Communion." I kept my promise five years later . . .[11]

Teasing and a Tantrum

Thérèse had exceptional spiritual insight at a young age, but in other ways she displayed the normal behavior of an ordinary child. In looking back over her youngest years, Thérèse recalled a certain May when she was still too young to attend evening devotions at church. She was left in the care of Victoire, a young woman who worked for the Martins. Victoire had a mischievous streak in her and occasionally liked to tease the younger girls, especially Thérèse. The earnest little Thérèse wanted to conduct Marian devotions at the May altar in her room. It was time for Thérèse and Victoire to begin the prayers and hymns, but the older girl kept teasing Thérèse. She wouldn't start the prayers. Instead, she just kept smiling, pretending not to hear Thérèse's entreaties. The little child was baffled. She felt the anger in her heart erupt as she pursed her lips and stamped her feet. Her cheeks were flushed, her eyes blazing. Victoire was stunned; she had never seen such a performance.

But even while she shouted and stamped her feet, Thérèse felt a flood of sorrow wash over her anger. She felt deeply repentant especially because Victoire had brought her two little candle ends for the service as a surprise. Victoire had gone overboard in her teasing, but for little Thérèse, that was not the point. She had let her temper run away with her.

First Confession

Thérèse had an acute sense of right and wrong for a young girl her age. She knew that she did not want to offend God. In fact, she wanted to grow in love for him. For this reason, she looked forward to her first Confession and prepared for it with a sense of excitement.

Thérèse was prepared well for her first Confession by her sister Pauline. Pauline had explained that the priest took the place of Jesus in this wonderful sacrament. Years later she wrote to Pauline:

> I made my confession in a great spirit of faith, even asking you if I had to tell Father Ducellier I loved him with all my heart as it was to God in person that I was speaking.[12]

Thérèse made her confession with confidence because Pauline had told her that the tears of Jesus would purify her soul.

Thérèse continued to receive the sacrament of Reconciliation before feast days "and it was truly a *feast* for me each time," she wrote.[13]

CHAPTER THREE

· · · · · · · · · · ·

Childhood Mysteries

Every member of Thérèse's family had a unique part to play in molding her personality. Each family member left warm memories of generosity and Christian witness. After her father, no one was so dear to the "little queen" as Pauline. During the time before Pauline's entrance into Carmel, she was there for Thérèse to answer her questions or to care for her during childhood illnesses.

Thérèse recalls wondering about the saints. They were all so different, she reasoned. Some had led long lives, others short lives. Some had been martyrs; others had lived faithfully as ordinary Christians. What happened to them in heaven? Were some happier than others? If those who had performed greater accomplishments received a glorious reward, would the saints of little deeds receive less? If this were the case, how could they be happy? Pauline would know about such things, Thérèse decided. Her older sister sent her into the dining room to find their father's large tumbler. Thérèse brought it back to Pauline who set it next to Thérèse's sewing thimble. Pauline filled both to the brim with water and asked her little sister to describe how full each object was. Both receptacles were completely full. Pauline "helped me understand that in heaven God will grant His Elect as much glory as they can take."[1]

The Lord spoke to the child Thérèse in ordinary ways: through the people around her, through the good books she read and reread, and through the holy pictures she had received from her teachers, especially one picture given to her by Pauline. Thérèse describes it as "the little flower of the Divine Prisoner." She wrote:

> Seeing that the name of Pauline was written under the little flower, I wanted Thérèse's name to be written there also and I offered myself to Jesus as His *little flower*.[2]

The flower image would reappear throughout Thérèse's life. She saw herself as frail as a flower, but singularly strong because of Jesus' love for her. She knew Jesus counts the birds, clothes the lilies, and takes care of the grass of the fields.

New Challenges

Thérèse left the secure confines of *Les Buissonnets* when she was eight and a half. Léonie had just finished her studies at the Benedictine school when Thérèse began her classes there. Céline, three and a half years older, was a student there too. While Thérèse had once been the more aggressive child, now the two children seemed to trade places. Céline had become more outgoing and Thérèse had grown more quiet, often on the verge of tears. Céline defended her younger sister at school. When they played school with their dolls, Céline's dolls were quite good while Thérèse's dolls were naughty at times and the teacher had to dismiss them from the classroom.

Needless to say, Thérèse did not adjust easily to her new environment. The close family life she had experienced and the security of being loved and accepted was all she had ever known. Now, Thérèse had neither Céline nor the Guerins to lend their support. A fellow classmate, an older girl who struggled in her studies, took a disliking to Thérèse, who was one of the youngest and brightest students in the class. "[S]he experienced a jealousy pardonable in a student," Thérèse wrote. "She made me pay in a thousand ways for my little successes."[3]

Thérèse continued to study well. She often excelled because of the quality of her home classes with Marie and Pauline. Her two older sisters had laid the scholastic framework on which their youngest sister could build. But the child who had lost her mother at the age of four was not the outgoing, vibrant girl who had once amazed her mother. Thérèse had grown into a shy and sensitive young lady. She suffered when she was the butt of mean words or actions. She suffered especially because she did not know how to defend herself. She cried easily and seemed to find communicating awkward. She felt a sadness, an aloneness that she could not share with anyone except Jesus. She could be herself with him alone and she spoke to him in her heart.

Thérèse's only relief and joy came when she walked home from school and the door of *Les Buissonnets* opened wide to welcome her. Her father's warm welcome and interest in her scholastic progress helped her to focus on the many good things that filled her daily life. "I would jump up on Papa's lap, telling him about the marks they were giving me, and his kiss made me forget my troubles."[4]

Pauline's Call to Carmel

Thérèse's often idyllic childhood was interrupted once again when her beloved Pauline began to discern a Carmelite vocation. Thérèse had once told Pauline of her desire to become a hermit, and her older sister had responded that she too wanted to be a hermit. Pauline then playfully promised to wait until her youngest sister was grown up so that they could go together. The sensitive child never forgot the promise.

One day, Thérèse overheard Pauline and Marie talking. Pauline spoke about entering the monastery. She would be joining the nuns at Carmel very soon. Thérèse was stunned. She understood what a monastery was. She had gone with her Father to the Carmelite chapel. Together they had prayed to Jesus in the tabernacle. They had seen the grille and he had explained that the nuns lived behind that enclosure. On the one hand, the nuns' life was mysterious and inviting to Thérèse. On the other hand, it would require of the child a gift greater than she could give at that time in her life. Once, as a four-year-old, she had stood looking up at her mother's coffin. She had kissed her mother's forehead and clung to her father's hand. Now she stared in her imagination at the monastery grille and imagined her precious Pauline, her second mother, disappearing behind it.

> I did not yet understand the *joy* of sacrifice. I was *weak*, so
> *weak* that I consider it a great grace to have been able to sup-
> port a trial that seemed to be far above my strength![5]

Pauline patiently explained her vocation to Carmel and what
it meant to her. It was not the building, or the nuns, or the daily
routine of prayer and work. It was a call from the Lord, an invitation to draw closer to him in a life of total consecration. Thérèse
listened intently and thought about her conversation with
Pauline. The girl turned the words over and over in her nine-
year-old mind. She pictured religious life as a garden, like the
well-kept backyard of *Les Buissonnets*. Close to nature, alive and
fresh, this garden offered an environment for healthy flowers and
plants to grow. Thérèse decided that she too would enter Carmel,
not "for *Pauline's sake*, but for *Jesus alone*."[6]

After Pauline entered the Carmel, the Martins and Guerins
were permitted a weekly half-hour visit. Thérèse and Céline usually only had a few minutes with their older sister. One Sunday
afternoon, Pauline arranged for Thérèse to visit Mother Marie de
Gonzague. Thérèse was delighted to see the prioress in person and
to be able to confide her desire to follow Jesus as a Carmelite. Marie
Guerin accompanied her cousin, but each of the girls spoke privately with the prioress at Thérèse's request. Mother Marie de
Gonzague told Thérèse she had a vocation, but that she would
have to wait until she was sixteen to begin her life in Carmel.

A Miraculous Cure

Thérèse was growing more aware of her own vocation to religious life, but this did not alleviate the pain she felt at Pauline's

departure. Thérèse had great difficulty adjusting to the sorrow of losing her second mother to Carmel. Her sorrow quickly expressed itself physically and she began to suffer from headaches and insomnia. She soon became so sick that she actually became bedridden for two months. She was aware of the conversations and activity around her, but she could not respond. Louis had Masses celebrated at Our Lady of Victories in Paris. During the novena of Masses, Marie knelt and prayed before the family statue of Our Lady. "A miracle was necessary," Thérèse said many years later, "and it was Our Lady of Victories who worked it."[7]

Marie asked the Blessed Virgin to cure her little sister, to release her from the powers of darkness. Even as she prayed, Thérèse's eyes became riveted to the statue. The tormented girl saw a smile form on the Virgin's face. Suddenly the pain and anguish that had locked her in seemed to melt away. She felt serenity and health flow back into her. The strange affliction was gone forever. Thérèse realized that she was cured.

Thérèse's complete cure from her mysterious illness brought with it a deep peace. The Virgin's smile was real, although she did not know why the Mother of God would have personally intervened in her life. The answer for Thérèse, of course, was that Mary is and always remains a mother. Thérèse no longer had her own mother or Pauline. But Thérèse had Mary who would always remain a vital part of her life and spirituality.

Chapter Four

. . . .

Moments of Grace

Thérèse continued to dream about Carmel, seeing many of her life experiences through the lens of one who intended to enter religious life. When she was ten years old Louis took his family back to Alençon for a two-week vacation—Thérèse's first opportunity to return to her first home. Seeing the city once more opened the wound of her mother's death. She pictured the coffin and the tears of her family. Her ears rang with her father's sobs and she felt loneliness again.

This vacation cast a new image of Alençon on Thérèse's mind. Thérèse witnessed the opposite ends of life's spectrum. The Martin's enjoyed their friends' villa, the parties, and the festivities. The vacation passed quickly. Caught up in innocent fun, Thérèse would still pull back during quiet moments and compare the comfortable lifestyle of the family in Alençon with her goal to acquire eternal happiness hereafter. She was only ten, but she realized that there were many more lessons to learn about life.

Several years later, thinking back on that vacation in Alençon, Thérèse reminisced in her *Story of a Soul*. She had gone to pray at her mother's grave and had asked her mother to protect her always. She wrote about the lessons she had learned and about the family they had stayed with in Alençon. She observed: "The friends we had there were too worldly; they knew too well how to ally the joys of this earth to the service of God."[1]

Thérèse mused that their friends did not think enough about the sure reality of death. Although still a child, Thérèse had tasted death. It had struck her to the core of her existence. Death and life were intimately tied together. They were welded into one experience of life for every human being. It would have been easy to get caught up in the comfortable and secure, but the dimension of the cross in the Gospel message was real. Thérèse would learn about the redemptive importance of suffering a little farther down the road on her spiritual journey.

First Communion Day

Thérèse continued to ponder the mysteries of life as she approached the precious day of her first Communion. Three months before the momentous occasion, Pauline gave Thérèse a book she had made to help her prepare for the special event. Thérèse fervently offered the little prayers and acts of virtue it suggested. Marie also gave her daily lessons. Thérèse felt that she had been thoroughly instructed and she waited anxiously for the day she would actually receive the Eucharistic Jesus.

During Thérèse's lessons, the girl paid close attention as Marie emphasized that the Christian vocation is an invitation from the Lord to walk with him and to grow in holiness. What most impressed the child was Marie's conviction that sanctity was made up of small matters. Making choices to please God, to please Jesus, could consist of small sacrifices, ordinary actions, such as doing tasks diligently. Whatever a person did as part of his or her daily life, if performed to please Jesus, was an act of love for him.

This realization—that holiness does not depend on the greatness of our actions, but rather on the love and power of God acting in us—was the concept that would grow in young Thérèse. The Lord would use her to remind the world once more that he is the God of love. This God of love is responsible for all the holiness that has ever been reflected in a human being since the beginning of time. Every saint, singled out by the Church as a model for imitation, owes his or her holiness to God. God is the initiator of all holiness, and he delights in his own reflection of goodness that a saint projects.

A saint is a mirror of the image of God. Yet all the saints put together cannot equal the love of God. Thérèse realized this early in her life. Her journey in holiness would not be a triumph of heroic actions. It would not be a triumph in the eyes of those around her. The Lord was to let her spend twenty-four years on this earth living a lesson, *being* a lesson, not teaching with words, except through her writings. She would live out her existence singing a hymn of ordinary words that were magnificent to the ears of the God who is Love because Thérèse's song was rooted in Love.

Thérèse's desire to become a saint—to become close to God—surfaced during this time of preparation for her first Communion. It deepened because of Marie's thorough explanations and the clarity with which Marie presented her own spiritual wisdom. Thérèse realized in this experience that sanctity or holiness is ordinary. As she grew in the spiritual life, she would further emphasize the beauty of offering little acts of love to God—not for a reward but in order to please him. She grew in the awareness that God is the Divine Lover of each human soul. She realized that no one, not even her father, or Pauline, or Marie, could ever love her as completely, as totally, as did God. This led her to abandon her life with trust to him. Perhaps this sounds so easy, so uncomplicated, like the feat of an athlete who makes his performance look effortless. As Thérèse walked in confidence with Jesus, she began to see her own image reflected in his loving gaze.

In 1884, Thérèse made a retreat at the boarding school. This was the immediate preparation for her first Communion. She treasured the spiritual conferences of Father Domin and copied down important points in her notebook. She appreciated the kindness of the nuns. During the retreat, Thérèse wore a large crucifix—a gift from Léonie—in her belt. This blessed object made her feel like a missionary.

First Communion day finally arrived. The class members, dressed in white, were led into church, while voices sang the hymn: "O blessed altar ringed with angels." It was a day of true joy for Thérèse. She believed that the Eucharist is God, her God, and that he was coming into her soul in a very special and intimate way for the first time. She wept blessed tears, not sad tears for the loss of her mother or with regret that Pauline could not be there. Her tears were the result of being overwhelmed by the Divine Lover of her soul.

In the afternoon the first communicants made the Act of Consecration to Mary. Thérèse felt the closeness of Our Lady. In early evening, Thérèse and her father walked to Carmel. Thérèse then watched as Pauline, wearing her white veil crowned with roses, professed her vows as a Carmelite nun. Then father and daughter walked back home. Papa gave Thérèse a watch for her First Communion gift. And the day came to an end, a beautiful day that Thérèse would never forget.

Christ Lives in Me

The next day was joyful, too. But Thérèse mused that her beautiful gifts and pretty dress were still not enough to satisfy her. She wanted to receive Jesus again in Holy Communion. As frequent Communion was not the custom in Thérèse's time, she was given permission by her parish priest to receive Communion on feast days. The next Church feast would be Ascension Day. The evening before each feast day, Marie would sit down with Thérèse and share with her the beauty of receiving the holy Eucharist. Thérèse listened attentively as her oldest sister spoke from her own experience about the power of Jesus in her life. On the Feast of the Ascension, Thérèse knelt at the railing with her father and Marie, and she whispered in her heart the words of Saint Paul, "It is no longer I who live, but it is Christ who lives in me" (Gal 2:20).

Thérèse continued to look forward to feast days when she could receive Jesus in the Eucharist and listen to Marie's lessons.

She vividly recalled one evening of preparation for Holy Communion when Marie talked to her about something that would remain burned into her soul.

> I remember how once she was speaking to me about suffering and she told me that I would probably not walk that way, that God would always carry me as a child.
>
> The day after my Communion, the words of Marie came to my mind. I felt born within my heart a *great desire* to suffer, and at the same time the interior assurance that Jesus reserved a great number of crosses for me. I felt myself flooded with consolations *so great* that I look upon them as one of the *greatest* graces of my life.[2]

A short while after Thérèse's first Communion, she received the sacrament of Confirmation. Bishop Hugonin of Bayeux confirmed her on June 14, 1884. She wrote:

> I was prepared with great care to receive the visit of the Holy Spirit, and I did not understand why greater attention was not paid to the reception of this sacrament of *Love*.[3]

The one-day retreat of preparation at the abbey was extended to two when the bishop was delayed. Thérèse was delighted to have more time to pray and prepare herself for the coming of divine Love.

Fitting In

After Confirmation, Thérèse resumed her normal activities and found herself at school with students who seemed not to be serious enough about their faith or studies. She felt uncomfortable with most of them. While she struggled to relate and to be accepted by her peers, she also wanted them to grow in maturity.

> I had a happy disposition, but I didn't know how to enter
> into games of my age level; often during the recreations, I
> leaned against a tree and studied my companions at a dis-
> tance, giving myself up to serious reflections![4]

Soon Thérèse found a way to manifest her more serious
approach to life. She and a few friends began to bury small dead
birds they gently gathered from around the property. The children surrounded the burials with appropriate ceremony. They
planted small shrubs and flowers to enhance the beauty of the
miniature cemetery.

Thérèse also tested her talents at storytelling. She invented a
story and added to it daily during recreation time. Her audience
grew, and that increased her confidence. In fact, she noted in her
Story of a Soul that sometimes even some of the older girls joined
the listeners. But then the teacher put a stop to bird burying and
storytelling. She wanted Thérèse and her friends to spend their
recreation time more actively.

Thérèse enjoyed learning and she grasped her lessons. She
excelled in catechism class. When Father Domin, the parish
priest, orally quizzed the students, Thérèse answered the questions without missing a word. When, on rare occasions, she
forgot an answer, tears would spill down her cheeks. The priest
appreciated her efforts and gently encouraged her. He called
Thérèse his "little doctor," presuming her to be named after Saint
Teresa of Avila, who was noted for her wisdom and holiness.

While in general Thérèse performed well in her classes, she
did struggle with some subjects. She described her handwriting
as a "terrible scrawl!" Thérèse also did not know how to seek out
admiration for what she did well. Her relatives, the Guerins,

thought of her as quiet and shy. At this time in her life, she was underestimated, even by those close to her. Though trying for young Thérèse, these difficulties were also opportunities for growth. With God's grace, Thérèse grew during this time and learned to become more indifferent to praise.

In her friendships with peers, Thérèse was loyal and manifested sensitivity to others' likes and dislikes. She would give her friends little inexpensive gifts that she treasured but wanted to give up to please them. She poured out her love and care on her family, relatives, and friends. Thérèse would one day channel her great love, making an offering of it at Carmel to the One who is the Source of all love.

· · · · · · · · · · · ·

CHAPTER FIVE

Growing in Freedom

As a young woman coming out of childhood, Thérèse would revert from time to time. However, God began to prepare her little soul so that she would gain greater interior freedom before entering Carmel.

In 1886, Marie followed in Pauline's footsteps by joining the Carmel at Lisieux. In the same year, Aunt Guerin invited Thérèse to stay a few weeks at the seashore. In the summer the Guerin family and Thérèse went to the seaside at Trouville. But without Céline, Pauline, Marie, Léonie, and, above all, her father, the vacation was no fun for Thérèse. She soon became lonely and homesick. After a few days, she had to return to *Les Buissonnets*. Where would she find the courage, only a few years later, to give her life to Jesus as a cloistered Carmelite religious? What power could transform this ordinary, homesick child into a person capable of giving her life totally to the Lord?

With Marie and Pauline gone, Thérèse could no longer rely on others in the way she once had. Thérèse struggled with loneliness, and she had particular difficulty with scruples. She would worry about what she had said or done, fearing that she may have sinned. Before, she had been able to work through her fears with the help of Marie, who listened to her anxious disclosures and calmed her little sister. Marie encouraged Thérèse to deepen her love for Jesus, who removes all fear. But after Marie entered Carmel, Thérèse had no one in whom she could confide her fears. She prayed to her four deceased little brothers and sisters and confidently asked them to help and uplift her.

In addition to her interior trials, God began to give Thérèse opportunities to mature in very small, practical ways. She wrote: "I had a great desire, it is true, to practice virtue, but I went about it in a strange way," she observed. Until she entered the convent, she "didn't do any housework whatsoever."[1] The family had hired help for domestic tasks. Thérèse recalls, however, that after Marie entered the convent, Céline took care of their bedroom. When Céline was away, Thérèse would make the bed and tidy the room. She noted that she did this for the love of God, but if Céline failed to realize or acknowledge Thérèse's act of love, she would feel hurt and shed tears. Acknowledging her extreme sensitiveness, Thérèse wrote: "God would have to work a little miracle to make me *grow up* in an instant."[2]

Christmas Eve Miracle

On Christmas Eve, December 25, 1886, the miracle that Thérèse needed occurred. With this one event, Thérèse would receive the grace she needed to emerge from childhood. She was with the family at Midnight Mass. In the crowded church, as the congregation sang Christmas carols and prepared to go back to their homes, Thérèse felt the power of Jesus touch her heart in a new way. He was offering her the opportunity to leave her childish ways behind forever. He was giving her the freedom to love him totally, to remain confident of his love, no matter what happened. He was offering her peace of soul.

For the first time in her memory, in an emotional moment, her eyes were dry. She had no tears. She felt peaceful and unafraid, convinced of the Lord's love for her.

That event followed that long and busy day. Her father felt tired as the family trudged home in the snow from Christmas Eve Mass. Céline was excited that, when they got home, as the family's youngest, she and Thérèse would still receive the traditional gifts in their shoes placed beside the fireplace. Louis would have appreciated going straight to bed, but the shoes were by the fireplace. "Well, fortunately this will be the last year!" he said.[3] Céline gasped softly. She knew Thérèse had heard their father's comment as they had gone upstairs together to remove their hats and coats. Céline expected a flood of tears from her little sister. "Oh, Thérèse, don't go downstairs,"[4] fearing that she would find the situation too hard to bear. But Thérèse understood her father's weariness. There was nothing for her to feel hurt about. Choking back her tears, she skipped quickly down the stairs and sat comfortably in front of the fireplace. One by one, she pulled the treasures from her shoes and proclaimed her joy. Louis, caught by the magic of the moment, forgot his fatigue and enjoyed Thérèse's delight.

Henri Pranzini

The Sunday after the miraculous moment on Christmas Eve, a holy card of Jesus crucified slipped out of Thérèse's missal. Her eyes fell on one of the Master's hands. It was pierced with a spike and blood was falling to the ground. The girl allowed her mind to penetrate the reality of the scene. She reflected that Jesus had spilled his blood for love of the people he came to redeem. But no one was there at the cross to catch that blood, to be cleansed by it.

Thérèse felt the desire to be there for Jesus, at the foot of his cross, to make reparation—especially for sinners who had grown hard and bitter. She seemed to hear Jesus say to her: "I thirst." Thérèse realized that his was no physical thirst. This thirst lay deep in the soul of the Savior, who longed for sinners to let him touch their hearts, cure their spiritual ills, and bring them to himself. Thérèse told Jesus that she wanted to help quench his thirst. She wanted to offer her prayers and sacrifices for the souls of great sinners. Was this what Jesus was asking of her? Perhaps he would give her a favorable sign.

Soon after, Thérèse learned of a man, Henri Pranzini, who had been condemned to death for grave crimes. He would be executed within days. Newspapers carried accounts of Pranzini's hardened attitude and the steel-like bitterness that closed in around him like a vice. Thérèse began to pray and offer sacrifices for Pranzini, whom she "adopted" as a spiritual child, someone she prayed for in a particular way. She talked Céline into going with her to the parish priest to arrange for the celebration of a Mass for Pranzini. The murderer's execution took place on August 31, 1887.

Thérèse had to know if her first spiritual child had shown some sign of repentance. She checked the newspaper the day after the execution for an account of what had happened. Paging through the *La Croix*, she quickly found what she was searching for. The condemned man had refused to go to confession before he had been taken to the scaffold. But a priest had stood quietly by, with a crucifix in his hands. The priest had watched anxiously for some sign that the man, so near death, would desire reconciliation with God. No sign came.

Then, the unexpected occurred. As Pranzini started to place his neck on the block, he looked up, turned his head toward the priest, and asked for the crucifix. Father quickly held it out and the man kissed it reverently, three times. Then the guillotine's blade hit its mark, and the repentant Pranzini was free.

Tears streamed down Thérèse's cheeks as she shared with Céline her secret and the story of Pranzini's conversion. As her first spiritual child, Pranzini would always be special to Thérèse. Jesus was pleased with her small sacrifices, with her prayers—and this was the sign she had hoped for, such a glorious sign. There was nothing that Jesus could not accomplish through her. Thérèse had learned a valuable lesson even though she was just fourteen years old.

With her growing love for Jesus and her desire to save sinners for the love of Jesus, Thérèse was freed from two of her own spiritual problems. Her scruples disappeared and she overcame her extreme sensitivity. Her sacrifices and prayers had helped to free Pranzini, and now she too was really free.

CHAPTER SIX

• • • • • • • • • • • •

Drawn to Jesus

Thérèse's growing maturity and freedom became evident in her daily life. She longed to be a channel of Jesus' love for the people of her time. She had developed a spiritual thirst to make Jesus known and loved. While she wanted others to love the Lord, her own love increased as well.

> I slaked His thirst and the more I gave him to *drink*, the more the thirst of my poor little soul increased, and it was this ardent thirst He was giving me as the most delightful drink of His love.[1]

Serene days lay ahead. Thérèse felt a deep interior joy. No longer tied down by anxiety and scrupulosity, her mind was free. She had always loved learning, but now she wanted to study useful subjects beyond what she was learning from her tutor, Madame Papinau. "I applied myself to some special studies in *history* and *science* and I did this on my own."[2] Thérèse pondered her study

habits and weighed her motives for studying in the light of
Scripture and the spiritual classic with which she was most familiar: *The Imitation of Christ*. In Ecclesiastes 2:11, Thérèse read:

> Then I considered all that my hands had done and the toil I
> had spent in doing it, and again, all was vanity and a chasing
> after wind, and there was nothing to be gained under the
> sun.

Thérèse also kept in mind chapter three of *The Imitation of
Christ,* which speaks of the right use of knowledge. She confined
her reading to certain times and hours to "mortify my intense
desire to know things."[3] One part of her felt pulled toward the
good things of this life; another part reached far beyond her
years to weigh circumstances in the light of eternity. She speaks
of being nourished on the pure flour of *The Imitation of Christ*
and the honey and oil of Father Charles Arminjon's *On the End
of the Present World and the Mysteries of the Future Life*.

Louis had borrowed Arminjon's book from the Carmelite
nuns, and Thérèse had asked to read it. She sat near the window
of her study and rested the book on the sill. Slowly she read the
book that spoke to her of the mysteries of faith and eternal life.
Thérèse was consoled by her belief in an afterlife. She was young,
but already could claim a big investment in that hope. Her
mother, as well as her two brothers and two of her sisters, were
alive in God. Paul wrote: "If for this life only we have hoped in
Christ, we are of all people most to be pitied" (1 Cor 15:19).
Thérèse weighed the greatness of eternal life with the sacrifices
that daily living would require of her. She came to the conclusion
that no matter what those sacrifices might be, they were worth
enduring with love if they lead to eternity with God.

Arminjon's reflections on the perfect love of God intrigued Thérèse. She felt her heart drawn as by a magnet to the heart of the Savior. "I wanted *to love, to love Jesus with a passion*, giving Him a thousand proofs of my love while it was possible."[4] She prayed to Jesus, letting the love he placed in her heart be her guide.

Spiritual Sisters

When very young, the three and a half years between Thérèse and her nearest sister, Céline, seemed great. Thérèse wanted very much to be a part of Céline's world, but Céline remained silent and aloof. She told her little sister that she would have to grow "'as high as a stool' so that she could have confidence in me."[5] Thérèse would climb up on the stool and beg Céline to let her in on her grown-up world, but still Céline refused. Then suddenly Céline's whole attitude toward Thérèse changed. Céline became trusting and open. She treated her youngest sister as an equal. The distance that had separated them disappeared.

Thérèse wrote: "Jesus, wanting to have us advance together, formed bonds in our hearts stronger than blood. He made us become spiritual sisters . . ."[6] Thérèse reflected in *Story of a Soul* that the friendship she and Céline experienced was the type spoken of by Saint John of the Cross in his *Spiritual Canticle*. The spiritual conversations the two sisters shared brought hours of delight to them both. Thérèse likened those precious times to the conversations Saint Monica had with her converted son, Saint Augustine. As the two saints spoke of their longing for heaven and the presence of God, it seemed as if they could experience some of the joy their faith told them they would find at their journey's end. Thérèse and Céline, in their young hearts, felt something of the same.

As the spiritual life grew in its attraction, Thérèse felt the desire to make little sacrifices and renunciations for the love of Jesus. Motivation was important to her. She wanted to do things *not* for a heavenly reward, but to please Jesus. At first, the renunciations cost her dearly. Sometimes, she admitted, her face betrayed her struggle. But as time passed, with the help of prayer and encouraged by Céline's efforts, Thérèse found joy in self-sacrifice.

At that time, too, she would have loved to receive Holy Communion daily, a privilege rarely given before the pontificate of Pope Saint Pius X (1903–1914). Thérèse received Communion as often as her confessor permitted, but she continued to believe in frequent Holy Communion. She prayed that the Church would not only permit daily communion but also foster it. That day would come not too long after her death. Thérèse's confessor invited her to receive the Eucharist four times a week during the month of May and added a fifth when a feast occurred. When the priest gave her this permission, she left the confessional with tears of gratitude streaming down her cheeks and a radiant smile. She could only think of the joy of receiving Jesus.

The Inner Call

Thérèse continued to feel an invitation within her soul, a call spoken by the Master. She had become attuned to Jesus, who was leading her so gently to himself. It seemed so clear to her though she was just fourteen years old: Thérèse would become a Carmelite nun. Like Pauline and Marie before her, she, too, felt drawn to Carmel.

Thérèse wanted to share her secret with Céline, but she was sensitive to the fact that Céline may also have been discerning a religious vocation. When Thérèse manifested her own desire, Céline realized that if Thérèse entered Carmel, the two great friends would be separated. Nevertheless, Céline encouraged Thérèse in every way. However, at Carmel Thérèse found some opposition in her sister Marie, who bluntly told Thérèse that she was too young. But Thérèse found solace in Pauline's encouragement.

Thérèse chose the feast of Pentecost to ask her father's permission to enter Carmel. It was May 29, 1887. She had turned fourteen in January. Thérèse found her father sitting at the edge of the well in the backyard garden. She sat next to him. Her eyes glistened with unshed tears. Her gentle father put his arm around his youngest child. "What's the matter my little Queen?" he asked.[7] They rose and walked slowly back and forth down the path, Thérèse's head resting on her father's strong chest. She told him of her desire to become a Carmelite nun, and she asked his permission to enter the convent as soon as possible. His tears mingled with his daughter's, but he didn't try to discourage her. Louis noted that she was very young, yet he knew the Lord would take care of her.

Louis went over to the garden wall and gently uprooted a small white flower from a crevice. He handed it to his little queen, and he explained that it was Jesus' love and care that had nurtured the flower until that very moment. Thérèse realized, by analogy, that she was like that little flower, cherished by Jesus and his heavenly Father. Thérèse took the flower and pressed it in her copy of *The Imitation of Christ*. She believed that the delicate flower would soon be transplanted to Carmel.

CHAPTER SEVEN

· · · · · · · · · · · ·

Seeking God's Will

Isidore Guerin, Louis's trusted advisor in family matters, was the next person in whom Thérèse confided her desire to enter Carmel. She approached him with the confidence his reaction would be similar to her father's. Unfortunately, her uncle was not in the same frame of mind. On October 8, 1887, Thérèse had a talk with him. "He forbade me to speak about my vocation to him until I was seventeen. It was contrary to human prudence, he said, to have a child of fifteen enter Carmel."[1] To impress his young niece with the seriousness of his decision, Isidore Guerin shouted that it would take a miracle for him to give his consent. Thérèse realized that prolonging her conversation with her uncle was useless. She slipped quietly out of the room and took her problem to Jesus in prayer. Her father had been the perfect person to start with. He had backed her, was there for her, made time for her, and showered her with the love of a father and a mother. Perhaps he could persuade her Uncle Guerin. But in her heart Thérèse knew that only God turns hearts around. She continued her prayers, asking Jesus with all her youthful confidence for a miracle.

Two weeks passed, which Thérèse referred to in *Story of a Soul* as "a long time."[2] Thérèse reflected on scriptural imagery that matched her mood and offered consolation. She pondered the anxiety of Mary and Joseph, who searched three days for Jesus before finding him in the Temple. From Wednesday, October 19, until Saturday, October 22, Thérèse felt unusually sad. Everything around her seemed to fade into night. She could not sense the nearness of Jesus. It felt as if he were hiding from her. The skyline of her soul was dark, without even a streak of light on the horizon. The weather matched her mood. Everything was gray. On Saturday, she went to the Guerins to visit, half hoping to talk to her uncle again about her vocation and half fearing to try.

Isidore Guerin greeted Thérèse as she visited with her cousins. Then he called her into his study. He began speaking gently, unlike their previous encounter. First he chided her for being afraid of him. Then he humbly told her that she would not have to beg for a miracle to change his decision about her vocation . . . "*the miracle had been granted* . . . he told me I was *a little flower God wanted to gather*, and he would no longer oppose it!"[3] The next day, Sunday, October 23, Thérèse paid a visit to Carmel to tell her sisters the wonderful news. She had her heart set on entering Carmel on the Christmas following her miraculous change of heart. Pauline, in her quiet way, broke the news that the superior of Carmel had said that she could not enter the Order until she was twenty-one.

The Carmelite nuns explained that Thérèse would have to be interviewed by the priest superior of the Carmelite community in Lisieux. On the agreed-upon date, she and her father were greeted by a straight-faced, soft-spoken priest who ushered them into his office. Louis looked reassuringly at his daughter, and Thérèse glanced from her father to the priest, searching anxiously for just a trace of welcome on the cleric's face. He was serious and succinct. Thérèse said that he "received us coldly."[4] The guests would hardly have had time to sit down.

Thérèse was much too young, the priest told her bluntly. Her father immediately spoke up in her defense, but the superior had made up his mind. He added, though, that if the bishop thought otherwise, he would have no more objections. The interview was over. The girl and her father had been treated as if they were interruptions in a very important schedule. There was nothing to do but leave, and they did, quietly, the old man's arm around his daughter's shoulder. Tears streamed down Thérèse's face. They went outside and quickly put up their umbrellas for protection against the pouring rain.

Louis reassured Thérèse and encouraged her on the walk home. He searched for words to console her. How many young people have a totally selfish outlook on life, he must have thought. All his little queen wanted was to follow her religious vocation. As they walked, Thérèse mentioned that she wanted to go to see the bishop in Bayeux. Her father promised to accompany her and support her. Louis Martin became as determined as his daughter. He promised to take her to the Holy Father, Pope Leo XIII, if it should prove necessary.

The Meeting with Bishop Hugonin

On October 31, 1887 Louis and Thérèse Martin journeyed to Bayeux to keep their appointment with Bishop Hugonin. As they approached the episcopal residence, which looked to Thérèse like a palace, she felt her former shyness enveloping her. If only her father would do the talking, but he had asked Thérèse to present her own request and explanation. She wished one or more of her sisters could be with her.

In Bayeux, the rain poured down in steady torrents. Louis Martin did not want his daughter to appear rain-soaked before the bishop, so they took a bus to the cathedral to wait until the rain had stopped. A large group of worshipers were attending a funeral as the Martins slipped into the first pew. Thérèse realized that in her bright dress and white hat she was a contrast to the black-clad mourners in the pews. After the funeral, she and her father waited in the small chapel behind the main altar for the rain to stop. When they could finally leave, Louis looked quickly around the cathedral's interior at the inspiring sight. But Thérèse could not focus on the church. She was on a mission. One part of her was overjoyed at the opportunity to plead her case. Another part of her dreaded the encounter.

The Martins went to the office of Father Reverony, the bishop's secretary who had made the appointment. Even though the priest had expected them, he was not there. Patiently, Mr. Martin took his daughter and toured the city on a bus. They had lunch and rested in a lovely hotel near the bishop's residence. When they returned a second time to Father Reverony's office, he was in. He brought father and daughter into his study and listened to

Thérèse's explanation of her reason for wanting to see the bishop. She was now almost there. Still Father Reverony had to make the visit happen. According to Thérèse's account, Father Reverony was kind and welcoming. He seemed surprised about the purpose of her wanting to see the bishop. But after asking a few simple questions, he said, "I am going to introduce you to the bishop; will you kindly follow me?"[5]

Tears rushed to Thérèse's eyes. Perhaps they were tears of relief. She would finally fulfill the purpose of her visit. Father Reverony suggested that she hide her tears from the bishop. They walked through several ornate rooms with large, comfortable-looking chairs. Portraits of bishops adorned the walls; Thérèse felt smaller and smaller as she and her father advanced toward the bishop's study.

Bishop Hugonin was the prelate of Bayeux and Lisieux (from 1867 until his death in 1898). He entered the room and the Martins kissed his ring. Thérèse sat in the big chair selected for her by Father Reverony. How she wished her father would explain the purpose of their visit, but she knew that this was her moment to speak. She gave her reasons for wanting to enter Carmel at her young age rather than having to wait until she was twenty-one. She was convinced and certain in her heart, but her own words sounded wooden and unimpassioned. She finished and looked anxiously at the prelate. The bishop asked Thérèse if she had wanted to enter the Carmelite convent for a long time.

"Oh, yes," Thérèse came back, "for a very long time."

"It couldn't have been fifteen years," Father Reverony smilingly interjected.

Thérèse blushed. "That's true," she responded, "but there aren't too many years to subtract because I wanted to be a religious since the dawn of my reason, and I wanted Carmel as soon as I knew about it. I find all the aspirations of my soul are fulfilled in this Order."[6]

The bishop gently suggested how consoling it would be for her father if Thérèse would remain at home for a few more years. But Louis Martin quickly came to his daughter's support and assured the bishop of his readiness to let his daughter enter then, at the age of fifteen. The bishop said that he would have to speak with the superior of Carmel in Lisieux. Thérèse felt beaten and drained. After all she and her father had been through on the journey to Carmel, were they to end back in the hands of Father Delatroette? Aware of the priest's adamant refusal, Thérèse's tears spilled over and slid uncontrollably down her cheeks. The bishop was moved. He put his arm around Thérèse and told her to have courage, to go on her pilgrimage to Rome and to rejoice because the trip to the Eternal City would strengthen her in her vocation.

The informal procession moved into the garden as they walked toward the gate. Louis Martin couldn't resist telling Bishop Hugonin that Thérèse had worn her hair piled neatly on top of her head in an attempt to appear older. The bishop was to tell that story many times later on when speaking of Thérèse.

Louis Martin then asked about a few details concerning the coming pilgrimage. Father Reverony would be guiding the pilgrimage, and he wanted specifics about what he and his two young daughters, Céline and Thérèse, should wear for the papal audience. The priest answered the questions and then accompanied Louis and Thérèse to the gate and shut it gently behind them.

Outside, the floodgates broke open and Thérèse sobbed on her father's shoulder. She was disappointed for herself, true, but also for her father who had planned to send a telegram to the Carmel of Lisieux announcing that the bishop had granted his permission for Thérèse to enter Carmel at fifteen. Years later she wrote of this sad event: "My soul was plunged into bitterness but into peace too, for I was seeking God's will."[7]

CHAPTER EIGHT

The Pilgrimage

Thérèse's sadness was mitigated by hope as she prepared for the upcoming pilgrimage to Rome in November. The big day finally arrived. Louis Martin and his two youngest daughters, eighteen-year-old Céline and fifteen-year-old Thérèse, blended in with the excited pilgrims at the Lisieux train station. They were to be there at 3:00 A.M. on that crisp November 4, 1887. The Martins were on time and fully awake. This special pilgrimage combined the pilgrims of two dioceses: Bayeux and the neighboring diocese of Coutances. The event was organized to honor Pope Leo XIII's fifty years of priesthood.

Pope Leo XIII had been elected to the See of Saint Peter in 1878. His twenty-five-year reign would span the new century and last until his death in 1903. The people who signed up for the pilgrimage felt a mixture of excitement and awe. They were going to travel to several famous cities as tourists, but more than that, they would be on a spiritual journey. The Martins felt that same excitement, but for Thérèse the journey had particular significance. Before she returned home to Lisieux, she would have met the Pope and spoken to him. Her heart beat faster at the thought of it. She pictured the audience in her imagination. She had seen portraits of Pope Leo XIII and could imagine him smiling at her and speaking with her. She could even hear his voice, a soft, calm voice like her father's.

The pilgrimage would conclude at the same train station nearly a month later. What adventures and excitement would fill that month! The itinerary of the French pilgrims would include stops in Paris, France, Switzerland, and various cities of Italy: Milan, Venice, Bologna, Loreto, Rome, Naples, Pompeii, Assisi, Florence, Pisa, and Genoa. They were to make a return visit to Pisa and Genoa before arriving back in Lisieux on December 2, 1887.

The train pulled into the Paris station in the morning. Louis Martin was anxious to show his girls the magnificent sites. They spent the next few days on their own and then joined up with the pilgrimage group on November 7. Thérèse enjoyed Paris, but what most impressed her was the shrine of Our Lady of Victories. Before the statue of the Blessed Virgin, Thérèse prayed earnestly to her heavenly mother. Her thoughts carried her back into the pages of her early life, when Mary had been especially near. After Thérèse's mother left this earth, Jesus' mother had cared for her. Thérèse felt the same gratitude toward Mary that she had experienced on her first Communion day five years earlier. Thérèse called her "Mama" and asked to be hidden *"beneath the shadow of her virginal mantle!"*[1] She asked

Mama to "keep far from me everything that could tarnish my purity." The Martins also visited the Basilica at Montmarte and consecrated themselves to the Sacred Heart of Jesus. Then they were ready for their journey.

On November 7, the pilgrims left Paris. They were directed to their seats on the train. Each of the cars was named after a saint. The Martins were assigned to the Saint Martin car, much to the delight of their father. The train started chugging down the track, slowly at first, then gathering speed. "Papa was very happy, when the train began to move he sang the old refrain, 'Roll, roll, my carriage, here we are on the open road.'"[2] The Martins made friends with the other pilgrims; they enjoyed the people and the people enjoyed them. Thérèse was delighted to feel at home and unafraid. "I was talking freely with the great ladies, the priests, and even the Bishop of Coutances."[3] This bishop led the pilgrimage. Thérèse recalled that when she would slip away into the group, her father, her king, would gently call her back and invite her to loop her arm through his, the way she did when they went on their walks in Lisieux. Bishop Hugonin's secretary, Father Reverony, was also a pilgrim. Thérèse noted in her autobiography that the priest was helpful and attentive to her and Celine throughout the pilgrimage. Frequently the priest would lean forward at the dinner table to better listen to Thérèse's conversation. By the end of the pilgrimage Father Reverony seemed convinced of Thérèse's call, but at the papal audience in Rome he would prove himself a stumbling block.

The train crept like a caterpillar through the mountains and valleys of Switzerland. Thérèse watched small villages with little cottages glide by. White clouds floated along. As the sun set across a large lake, the water shimmered in the reflection. This panorama of nature's beauty etched itself deeply into Thérèse's memory.

Stepping Stones to Rome

Milan was their first stop in Italy on the way to Rome. The pilgrims gazed at the magnificent white marble cathedral. They climbed the steps and entered to view the interior. Statues of saints "formed a small population."[4] Huge pillars held up the structure and dwarfed the travelers. The Martins stayed close to the bishop to hear his explanation of the saints' relics. They participated in his Mass at the tomb of Saint Charles Borromeo, once the bishop of Milan. Those who were physically able climbed to the top of the bell tower and stepped onto the roof, scanning the city below. People walking along the streets seemed as tiny as insects.

After the cathedral, the pilgrims were taken on the first of a series of tours. They stopped at a unique cemetery called Campo Santo. The marble statues that marked the graves were lifelike carvings of individuals performing tasks reflecting how they made their livelihood. Thérèse noticed a statue of a child scattering flowers on the grave of its parents. The petals were so life-like that they seemed to float in the breeze. Belief in heaven, in an afterlife, was evident in the city's churches and monuments that spoke eloquently of the faith of the people who revered them.

The pilgrims went on to Venice, city of waterways and gondoliers, then to Padua where the Martins venerated the relics of Saint Anthony of Padua. Next they traveled to Bologna where they prayed before the remains of Saint Catherine of Bologna. After an unsettling encounter in the crowded train station, where a young man tried to drag her away from her family (an incident Thérèse alludes to only briefly in her autobiography), Thérèse was anxious to depart for the next stop on the journey: Loreto.[5] There the Martins toured the Holy House that has long been venerated as the home of the Holy Family miraculously transported to Loreto from Nazareth. Thérèse and Céline left their father with the tourists to participate in a Mass at the main altar of the basilica. The two sisters found a priest who, by special privilege, was celebrating Mass in the Holy House itself. Thérèse and Céline asked the priest if they could receive Communion at his Mass. He immediately asked for two small hosts. The Martin girls knelt devoutly as the priest began the Eucharist. Then at Communion time, they received their Lord. Thérèse remembered the event so vividly nearly ten years later as she wrote in her *Story of a Soul* that it seemed to have happened just a few days before.

The pilgrimage continued on schedule. The next part of the journey would bring them to Rome.

Rome at Last

The pilgrims' train pulled into Rome's train station late at night. The passengers woke to the porters' shouts announcing their arrival in the city of popes and martyrs. The Martins looked forward to spending eight days in the eternal city. Thérèse clung to the most exciting dream of all: her visit with Pope Leo XIII that would take place on the seventh day.

The first day in Rome the Martins and the other pilgrims toured the outskirts, taking in the impressive Roman monuments. Thérèse noticed the peacefulness of the countryside, uncluttered by commercial influence. Parts of the city of Rome, on the other hand, were marked by something of a secular atmosphere, reminding her of Paris.

During the coming days, Thérèse and Céline were dazzled by the sights, especially by the Coliseum. While their father stood attentively listening to the tour guide, his girls slipped under the construction barricade and descended into the arena. They searched for and found the stone with a cross etched into it, hallowing the spot where many martyrs had given their lives for Jesus.

Thérèse writes in her *Story of a Soul*:

> My heart was beating hard when my lips touched the dust stained with the blood of the first Christians. I asked for the grace of being a martyr for Jesus and felt that my prayer was answered![6]

As the two girls rejoined the group of pilgrims, Louis nodded and smiled. How could he be upset at the fervor of his impulsive daughters?

The pilgrims toured the catacombs, and Thérèse took some earth from the tomb of Saint Cecilia as a relic of the martyred saint. Thérèse was thrilled to actually stand in Cecilia's tomb. She also visited the saint's home, the site of her martyrdom. The pilgrims learned that Cecilia had been proclaimed patroness of music by the Church. This was not because she played an instrument or sang beautifully, but because she had sung a song to Jesus, the Spouse of her heart, when she was being martyred.

Thérèse and Céline were impressed by this heroine. They were attracted by her virginal love for the Lord. They too wanted to sing a song to their Spouse, to give him their hearts. "I felt more than devotion for her; it was the *real tenderness of a friend*."[7] The Martins then visited the Church of Saint Agnes, Agnes being Pauline's religious name in Carmel. Meanwhile, the days passed and Thérèse's excitement and anxiety mounted as Sunday's papal audience drew near.

The Papal Audience

The pilgrims gathered in the papal chapel for Mass at 8:00 A.M. Pope Leo XIII moved reverently through the Mass. He was prayerful and intent. Thérèse could hardly take her eyes off him. Her thoughts raced ahead to the audience that would follow. Her pulse beat more quickly and her cheeks burned. At Communion time, she poured out her anticipation to Jesus, really present within her. He understood; she knew he did. And very soon, in minutes, she would be able to voice her simple request to the pope. She glanced over at Céline whose eyes met hers in a quick, knowing look. Everything seemed to be a sign from God of his special interest and concern. The Gospel of the Sunday liturgy was proclaimed: "Do not be afraid, little flock, for it is your Father's good pleasure to give you the kingdom" (Lk 12:32).

After Mass, the pilgrims formed a line and knelt one by one before Pope Leo XIII, kissing his slipper and his ring. The pope in turn blessed each one. Thérèse's turn came. Moments before, Father Reverony, in a solemn tone, announced to the group that none of the pilgrims was to speak privately to the pope because time was at a minimum. Thérèse felt panic racing through her. She turned to Céline who was behind her. "What should I do?" she whispered. "Speak," Céline said decisively.

Thérèse stepped forward and knelt before the pope. She kissed the Holy Father's slipper and ring. Blotting out the stern face of Father Reverony at the pope's side, she leaned forward. Her innocent gray eyes pierced the heart of Pope Leo XIII, who instinctively leaned forward to listen. She gazed up at him and blurted out in one sentence the only request she had of the Church: "Holy Father, in honor of your jubilee, permit me to enter Carmel at the age of fifteen!"[8] What passed through the pope's mind when he looked at this young woman? How different were their paths in life. Leo XIII would be one of the longest-reigning popes in history: from 1878 to 1903— twenty-five years. Thérèse would live just twenty-four years and nine months. She knelt before him just as she was: a person with a sense of urgency. She seemed to know that she didn't have much time.

Father Reverony told the Holy Father that Thérèse was a child who wanted to enter Carmel at the age of fifteen. He could have reinforced her request, but he did not. Resting her folded hands on the pope's knees, Thérèse made a final impassioned plea. "Oh! Holy Father, if you say yes, everybody else will agree!"[9] The pope gazed intently down at her. "Go . . . go. . . . *You will enter if God wills it!*" he responded.[10] Thérèse tried to speak again, but Pope Leo XIII placed his index finger over her lips. Two guards appeared out of nowhere. Gently, efficiently, they took an elbow each and lifted Thérèse across the room and into the waiting area. Tears blinded her eyes.

The audience of Louis Martin and the other men followed that of the women. Louis Martin was introduced by Father Reverony as the father of two Carmelite nuns. Pope Leo XIII was impressed and placed his hand affectionately on his head. Thérèse's father glowed as he thought of Marie and Pauline, his two oldest children, united with them in spirit. Oh, if Zelie could only be there to share in the joy of that moment. Yet something told him that she was there. She did know. Two regal papal guards assisted Louis as they had each pilgrim, guiding them to the adjoining waiting room.

After the audience, Thérèse calmed down and renewed her trust in Jesus. Whatever God wanted, she wanted, and she knew he would give her the grace to believe in that prayer. Jesus was silent as Thérèse and her family left the Vatican. The tears continued to stream down her cheeks, but Thérèse was at peace. She stepped out with her father and Céline into the pouring rain.

The Pilgrimage Concludes

What did Jesus want of Thérèse? At this point in her young life, she could give him her total trust. She prayed a prayer expressing her faith and trust and felt renewed strength. There was a reason for everything; she knew that. And even though she could not see beyond the roadblocks that seemed to prevent her from following her dream, she believed everything would ultimately work out. To doubt that would be to doubt Jesus himself, and that was unthinkable. She remembered the account of Jesus being asleep in the boat and the apostles' fear of drowning in the storm. The Lord was asleep in Thérèse's boat too. But she trusted that he would awake and take matters into his sure hands.

The pilgrims traveled on to Naples, Pompeii, and Assisi. It was in Assisi that Thérèse lost the buckle on her dress. While she searched for it, the carriages pulled away. She was left behind with the last carriage of the pilgrimage. Thérèse looked up at the passengers and her face turned crimson. The carriage belonged to the intimidating Father Reverony, the very last person in the world Thérèse wanted to ride with. All the passenger seats were taken, but one gentleman quickly jumped out and joined the driver, and Father Reverony invited Thérèse to enter.

As the carriage bounced along, the priest went out of his way to be gracious and pleasant. He no longer wore the stern look that he had maintained during the papal audience. His voice was kind and respectful. He chatted with Thérèse on an adult level. When the carriage arrived at the station, the wealthy passengers pulled out their large purses and opened them to tip the carriage driver. Thérèse looked around at the important people and felt she should do the same. She opened her purse and found some coins. Father Reverony gently told her not to think of it. He paid for both Thérèse and himself.

The pilgrims stopped in Florence, then passed once more through Pisa and Genoa on their way home to France. They arrived back in Lisieux on the afternoon of December 2, 1887. This pilgrimage would always be remembered by Thérèse, who just ten short years later would enter eternity. Yet in the decade that remained to her, the Lord would accomplish great things in Thérèse's soul. In a sense, Thérèse's vocation began at the feet of Pope Leo XIII and lingered at the nailed feet of the Crucified.

But that would not be the whole of the journey, although Thérèse's life was marked with the cross. Her story would end in victory, sealed in the glory of Jesus.

· · · · · · · · · · · ·

CHAPTER NINE

Gaze Set on Carmel

When Thérèse returned from her pilgrimage, she went to visit the nuns at Carmel. So much had happened since her last visit. Louis Martin had just offered her the opportunity to go on another pilgrimage, this time to Jerusalem. But Thérèse had quickly declined. While the thought of the Holy Land was appealing, the invitation had come too soon. She had just experienced one train ride, one coach ride too many. She wanted nothing other than to walk firmly on solid ground and to enjoy Lisieux's familiar streets. Thérèse's desire to enter Carmel as soon as possible and to continue her pilgrimage to heaven was far more important to her than earthly pilgrimages.

She visited Carmel and was particularly grateful for the time she could pour out her thoughts and adventures—a whole month's worth—to Pauline. Now what more could Thérèse do to obtain permission to enter Carmel? Pauline suggested that

Thérèse write to Bishop Hugonin to remind him of his promise to contact her about the matter. Thérèse went home and did as Pauline suggested. Isidore Guerin felt that her letter was too simple. He helped her to draft another. Just when they were going to mail it, Thérèse received a message from Pauline to hold on to it for a few days. On December 15, the letter was finally mailed. Thérèse longed for the bishop's instant reply. She wanted to spend that Christmas at home in Carmel.

Every morning after Mass, Louis patiently accompanied Thérèse to the post office. Each day brought another disappointment—no letter from the bishop. Christmas drew nearer. Louis's heart ached for his youngest child. Perhaps his heart ached a little for himself, too. What would the first Christmas without his little queen be like?

Glimpse of a Carmelite Christmas

But Christmas would come and go as it always had. Jesus wanted Thérèse to be home at *Les Buissonnets*; that is where he would find her. Thérèse thought of it as if the child Jesus had fallen asleep. His toys were left untended in a corner. He still loved the toys, but because he was a real human as well as a divine child, he had the needs of a child. And so he slept. He took his nap while Thérèse waited for him to wake.

After Midnight Mass, the Martins returned home to continue their celebration of the Savior's birth. When Céline and Thérèse made their way to their room, Thérèse was greeted with a delightful surprise. Artistic Céline had decorated a washbasin to give the appearance of a little pond. She had crafted a sailboat and placed it in the center. The boat contained an image of the child Jesus holding a ball in his hand. The sail of the boat had a hand-painted message from Scripture: "I sleep, but my heart watches" (Song 5:2). On the side of the boat was the word *abandonment*.

On Christmas afternoon, the Martins paid a short visit to Carmel. When the curtain covering the grille opened, Thérèse's eyes fixed on the infant Jesus. He held a ball in his hand, symbolic of Thérèse's expression that she was a toy of Jesus that could be lavished with attention or forgotten. The ball had Thérèse's name on it. Then the nuns sang a hymn for her that had been composed by Pauline. Thérèse was overwhelmed by their thoughtfulness. She exclaimed her gratitude through a steady stream of tears.

The Final Delay

On January 1, 1888, a letter was delivered to Thérèse. It was from Mother Marie de Gonzague who informed Thérèse that the bishop's permission for her immediate entrance to Carmel had arrived at Carmel on December 28, 1887. Mother de Gonzague explained that she had decided to delay telling Thérèse until January 1. But there was more. Mother had also decided that Thérèse should not enter until after Lent, which would mean a delay of three more months. Although Thérèse could not assume the reasons or dare to ask, it would seem logical that the prioress wished to spare the young applicant the challenges of a Carmelite Lent.

Time passed. Thérèse particularly treasured the days she still had with Céline. The girls shared spiritual conversations and good times together. Thérèse wanted to spend her remaining months preparing to enter Carmel. In *Story of a Soul* she presented her approach to self-denial and mortification. She explained that she never performed heroic penances of which great saints were capable. Thérèse wrote simply that she was never attracted to severe mortifications. Instead she revealed:

> My mortifications consisted in breaking my will, always so ready to impose itself on others, in holding back a reply, in rendering little services without any recognition, in not leaning my back against a support when seated, etc., etc. It was through the practice of these *nothings* that I prepared myself to become the fiancée of Jesus, and I cannot express how much this waiting left me with sweet memories.[1]

Saying Goodbye

The distance from *Les Buissonnets* to Carmel was short even on foot. But what a long journey it had been for fifteen-year-old Thérèse. The night before she entered the convent, her family and close relatives shared a meal and evening together. Thérèse was touched by the love and affection each showed her. Their confidence in the maturity of her decision meant so much to her.

Louis was quiet, but he gazed at Thérèse often. Where had the years gone? If only Zelie could be there now for this wonderful moment. He couldn't help but realize the loneliness he would bear after the departure of his youngest daughter. Yet her happiness made it worth the personal loss. That was his approach to all his children. But life was going to be much more ordinary without Thérèse. No more frantic walks to the post office. No more tears or visits to Bishop Hugonin. No more pilgrimages, or afternoon walks, or picnics, or Eucharistic visits with his little queen. Louis's memory was filled with a panorama of events that he would always treasure.

The next morning Thérèse linked her arm in her father's just as she had done so often in years gone by. Her family and relatives met for Mass at the monastery chapel and received Communion. As they prayed in thanksgiving, they wept. It was a wonderful day and yet also a sad day. Goodbyes are always hard. And even though Thérèse would live near them in the same town, the cloistered life she was choosing would restrict them from seeing her. It was true that when Thérèse left *Les Buissonnets* on April 9, 1888, she would never see her home again.

From the chapel, Thérèse and Louis went to the enclosure door. There, Thérèse knelt and asked her father's blessing. He carefully traced the sign of the cross on her forehead. Then he helped her up. While they hugged, they wept. This was the hardest part of all: to leave her Papa, her king, in order to find the King of kings.

Chapter Ten

The Carmel of Lisieux

The doors of Carmel closed and Mother Marie de Gonzague came forward to embrace Thérèse. Then her sisters Pauline and Marie hugged her. Thérèse could hardly believe she had finally arrived. She looked around the softly lit hallway and wondered what the rest of the monastery was like. She was just beginning her religious life as a postulant.

Thérèse was led to the nun's chapel, called the choir. The Blessed Sacrament was exposed. The choir was dim so that the worshipers on the public side of the grille could adore the Eucharist but would be unable to see the nuns. Thérèse remembered so vividly the times she and her father had come to pray there during their afternoon walks. First Pauline, then Marie had gone behind the grille. *What was behind it?* Thérèse had wondered. It was so mysterious and exciting. As the years had passed, and much too slowly at that, Thérèse had begun to realize the beauty of the life Pauline and Marie had chosen. At the heart of their vocation was a person, the person of Jesus. What a marvelous call they had received: to be brides of Christ.

Thérèse's eyes met the gaze of Mother Genevieve, who was in adoration before the Blessed Sacrament. Thérèse knelt next to her for a moment and experienced the awareness that she was with a saint. Mother Genevieve of Saint Thérèse (1805–1891) had founded the Lisieux Carmel in 1838. Thérèse wrote: "I remained kneeling for a moment at her feet, thanking God for the grace He gave me of knowing a saint . . ."[1] Then Thérèse left the choir and followed Mother Marie de Gonzague on a tour of the monastery. She felt an excitement fused with peace and calm.

Thérèse joined in the rhythm of monastic life. While everything was new, and for her nothing could be considered routine, her approach to the daily living out of her decision to enter Carmel reflected a maturity beyond her years. She felt that she had a realistic grasp of what her life would consist of for as long as she would live. "I found the religious life to be *exactly* as I had imagined it." She found more thorns than roses. "Yes," she said, "suffering opened wide its arms to me and I threw myself into them with love."[2] Thérèse felt that the Lord was calling her to suffer for the spiritual needs of those for whom he died. She was especially sensitive to the Carmelite vocation to pray for priests. As she began her life at Carmel, the young postulant made sure to keep her sufferings to herself. She was determined that the sisters would not be able to detect a tear or a frown. She was serene.

The Guidance of Father Pichon

Thérèse's oldest sister, now Sister Marie of the Sacred Heart, pronounced her vows on May 22, 1888. The Jesuit priest, Father Almire Pichon, came for the profession ceremony. Much earlier in Thérèse's autobiography she referred to the torment she had carried in her heart for about five years, from the time of her mysterious illness at age ten to her sister Marie's profession. Now Father Pichon helped the new postulant to make a general confession. He listened compassionately as Thérèse poured out her weaknesses and sins. She tried earnestly to be as sincere as she could be. Most of all, she seemed to have felt the nagging guilt that she could have possibly been responsible for her own illness as a child of ten.

Father Pichon grasped the anxiety in Thérèse's soul. He could see her sincerity and desire to grow and mature in the spiritual life. But Thérèse does recall that Father Pichon considered her fervor to be childish and her spiritual journey very sweet. Speaking of her confession to Father Pichon, Thérèse writes: "... the *Father* of our souls, as with a wave of his hand, removed all my doubts. Since then I am perfectly calm."[3]

At the end of her confession, Father Pichon assured her that she had never committed a mortal sin. He said:

> "Thank God for what He has done for you; had He abandoned you, instead of being a little angel, you would have become a little demon.... My child, may Our Lord always be your Superior and your Novice Master."[4]

These last words deeply moved Thérèse and she would later note that Jesus was her true spiritual director.

Father Pichon was transferred to Canada in 1888. Thérèse considered him to be her spiritual director, so his transfer was a disappointment. Just the same, Thérèse wrote to him every month. Father Pichon answered her correspondence with one letter a year. He really had left her to the Lord, the perfect novice master.

The Way Grows Steep and Rocky

The Lord continued to guide Thérèse along the path of holiness in Carmel, and she followed him willingly. Thérèse had no illusions about the challenges of the day-to-day living of religious life. It was not going to be easy, but she wasn't asking for an easy life. The unavoidable difficulties came.

First of all, the austere lifestyle was challenging to a teenager who had experienced little hardship. The sisters rose at 5:30 A.M. and retired at 10:30 P.M. They came together to recite the Divine Office in the choir at morning, mid-day, and evening. They also spent two hours daily in private prayer. There were two periods of community recreation, after dinner and after supper. Breakfast was a very light meal; on fast days something to drink and a piece of dry bread. The remainder of the day was spent in doing household tasks or other manual work, always in silence and, as much as possible, in solitude.

Thérèse liked the community and blended in nicely. The painful days of her childhood spent on the fringes of loneliness at the Benedictine school were no more. Thérèse's outgoing personality, sensitive and cheerful, caused several of the Carmelites to value her presence and to cherish her as a gift to the community. But there were challenges to face as well. However, Thérèse believed suffering to be an inevitable part of the human condition, a Christian's sharing in the cross of Jesus—and she was no stranger to conflict and suffering. Although she had grown up in a loving family environment, Thérèse's experience at boarding school had its share of pains and happy times. Thérèse realized that the Lord's invitation to holiness in community could be found through her loving acceptance of a sharp word, an impatient glance, an insinuating remark.

Although she had been her father's little queen at *Les Buissonnets*, she was not a queen at Carmel. In her early convent days, when difficulties arose, Thérèse must have been tempted to run to Pauline and Marie, who were like mothers to her. But she did not permit herself to do this. She forced herself to adhere to the rules and protocol of her Order because she believed that the Lord wanted this sacrifice of her.

Mother Marie de Gonzague had accepted Thérèse willingly into Carmel. When Thérèse was just nine years old, Mother de Gonzague had said that Thérèse had a vocation to Carmel, although she would have to wait until she was sixteen. Although the prioress could be delightful and gracious with Thérèse, she could also be very stern. Thérèse admits that during her postulancy, she couldn't meet Mother de Gonzague without having to kneel down and kiss the floor—as an act of humility—for some mistake or infraction of the Rule. In her autobiography, Thérèse recalls the cobweb she missed while sweeping the dimly-lit hallway. In front of all the nuns, Mother de Gonzague said: "We can easily see that our cloisters are swept by a child of fifteen! Go and take that cobweb away and be more careful in the future."[5]

Thérèse recognized that she often displeased the prioress. She realized that she was very slow in completing her duties and that she needed to become more thorough. But Thérèse was perplexed. It was helpful to be told, but she wanted to be shown *how* to improve. This was what her novice mistress did.

Being corrected occasionally in front of the community was humiliating, but another challenge hurt more. The novice mistress, Sister Marie of the Angels, sent Thérèse daily during nice weather to weed the convent garden. The novice mistress was "really a saint," according to Thérèse. Sister Marie of the Angels must have realized how much a new postulant would appreciate being outdoors among the flowers and shrubs. That part of the assignment was delightful. The other side of the coin was that Mother de Gonzague usually passed by in late afternoon. It was inevitable that Thérèse would meet her. The postulant records in her *Story of a Soul* some biting words from the prioress: "Really, this child does nothing at all! What sort of novice has to take a walk every day?"[6] The treatment Thérèse received from Mother de Gonzague in no way resembled the gentle compassion of her father and sisters. But as difficult as their relationship became, Thérèse demonstrated a profound understanding of the mother prioress and a sincere love for her.

Spiritual Life at Carmel

Within the Carmelite Order of Thérèse's era, two basic approaches to the spiritual life coexisted: mystical spirituality and ascetical spirituality. Mystical spirituality, as lived by Saint John of the Cross and other great mystics, held love to be the essence of the spiritual life. It focused on God primarily as Love. Mother Genevieve, the foundress of the Lisieux Carmel, lived this spirituality. Along with her, Mother Agnes of Jesus (Thérèse's sister Pauline) and Thérèse were at home in that spiritual ambiance. The other approach to the spiritual life, the ascetical spirituality, predominated in Thérèse's time. The ascetical thrust was to see God primarily as a judge. According to this tradition, a person's spiritual focus was on making reparation, saving souls, and performing extraordinary penances. Mother Marie de Gonzague favored this approach to the spiritual life.

Mother de Gonzague was simply being herself. She walked through the pages of Thérèse's life causing a flurry at times, and yet the focus of Thérèse's story remained. Thérèse demonstrated that she could learn positive lessons from everyone she met. Thérèse was genuinely grateful for the good done her and truly forgiving of those who hurt or insulted her.

As the days of Thérèse's postulancy passed, adjusting to her new life was not the only challenge. Louis Martin's health was deteriorating rapidly. He suffered a stroke on May 1, 1887. On June 23, 1888, he became disoriented and wandered away from home. While his Carmelite daughters prayed, Céline and Isidore Guerin searched for Louis Martin. They found him on June 27 in La Havre. On August 12, Louis suffered another stroke, this time at *Les Buissonnets*. On October 31, he suffered still another serious relapse. His recovery was slow, but steady.

Louis Martin's heart was set on visiting his daughters at Carmel. He was determined to be there on January 10, 1889, when his little queen would receive the religious habit. Nothing would keep him away—not even a legion of strokes.

CHAPTER ELEVEN

The Bride

From January 5 through January 10, 1889, Thérèse prepared for the day when she would receive the religious habit of Carmel. She tried to keep her mind focused on the seriousness of her retreat, but her heart fluttered with excitement just the same. Her father would be present to share her joy, as he had always been there for her in the happy times, in the sad times, in the everyday times. It seemed for so long that her father might not recover from his illnesses, but he did, and he would be there, the proud father, to give his Thérèse away.

Bishop Hugonin would officiate, which would add solemnity to the ceremony. Thérèse smiled as she remembered what she had gone through, what her father had gone through, and, for that matter, what the bishop had gone through to enable her to follow her call. Thérèse had not received her wish to enter Carmel for Christmas 1887, but she realized in time that the three-month delay had been spiritually enriching. In fact, she remarked how that March of 1888 had been "one of the most beautiful months of my life."[1] Thérèse had learned to wait and to deepen her trust in the Lord.

Clothing Day

It was Bishop Hugonin who selected January 10, 1889 as the day for Thérèse's reception of the habit. On that same day Thérèse would begin the next stage of her religious formation: the novitiate. The evening before, she gazed out of the monastery window. The courtyard was gray and barren. A light drizzle was falling. Thérèse's imagination traveled to the chapel that would look so bright and festive the next day; then back to the cloister courtyard—a bleak patch of earth in the misty shadows.

Thérèse was thrilled to think that she would be surrounded by her father and sisters, as well as by the Guerins, at the ceremony. Could she possibly ask the Lord for one more little favor? And for him, the Lord of heaven and earth, it would truly be a little favor. It didn't hurt to ask. Snow. If only she could have snow.

The mild weather continued the next morning. Thérèse had to admit that snow would be highly unlikely, but that was fine too. The moment for the celebration arrived and she felt excited and happy. Dressed in her bridal gown and veil, Thérèse's sandy curls hugged the rim of the veil's crown then fell in natural ringlets to her shoulders. Her pink cheeks glowed, a combination of robust health and excitement. Her deep-set eyes were alert, anxious to see her father.

It was time for Thérèse to step out of the cloister into the entrance where Louis Martin and the family waited. As he hugged his youngest daughter, Louis Martin's eyes shone bright. How proud he was of her, so grown up, so in love with her calling. He seemed once again to be his former, healthy self. The strokes were forgotten. He felt like the much younger father he had once been when he and Thérèse had taken their daily afternoon strolls, visiting local churches to adore the Blessed Sacrament. Happy memories crowded his mind—the Sunday walks to Mass when little Thérèse had clung proudly to his hand, the family recreations before the fireplace.

Today Thérèse's lips smiled while her eyes shimmered with tears. She was happy and sad, laughing and crying all at once. How she had missed her father, yet now he was here, for this wonderful though brief occasion. The bishop was ready. It was time to begin. Thérèse took her father's arm so simply and surely. He patted her hand affectionately. Together they walked down the aisle, slowly, in step. Louis beamed and Thérèse looked modestly up at him. The joy on his face was transparent. The sisters sang and Bishop Hugonin moved the ceremony reverently ahead.

Thérèse reflected on her father's generosity with God. He had given all his children to the Lord. Céline had recently confided to her father her desire to enter Carmel. Léonie, too, was convinced of her religious vocation. She would just take longer to settle into her life as a Visitation nun. All his children were a consolation for him. But Thérèse was a realist. Her father's health was precarious. Today could be considered, in comparison to Jesus' life on earth, as the Palm Sunday triumph before the Passion. Thérèse felt as if the pain and humiliation caused by the weight of his illness were stalking her father. Whatever suffering her father would bear would be just as much her suffering, and that of her sisters. If only she could spare him the least amount of grief. If only she could take his sickness upon her own healthy shoulders. But that would be up to her Spouse.

At the conclusion of the celebration the bishop introduced an unplanned addition. He solemnly intoned the *Te Deum*, a hymn of thanksgiving to God usually sung when religious pronounced their vows. After the ceremony, Thérèse left chapel and embraced her father. He was tired, but at peace. Thérèse's eyes followed him as he slipped out of the door onto the walkway with her other relatives. The young nun's eyes burned as she reentered the cloister and came face to face with the prominent statue of the Child Jesus. Could it be smiling only at her? Her father's departure seemed to settle more peacefully in her heart. Then an unusual brightness caught Thérèse's eye. She glanced beyond the statue into the cloister garden. It was completely covered with snow!

Bishop Hugonin came into the cloister after the ceremony and visited with the community. The sisters and the priests who had accompanied the bishop now heard the story of Louis and Thérèse Martin's trip to the bishop's residence in Bayeux. Bishop Hugonin enthusiastically described the way Thérèse had piled her hair on top of her head to look older. Thérèse felt her cheeks blush. She enjoyed the mirth, even if it was at her expense. When the guests had gone and the cloister resumed its normal routine, Thérèse reviewed the events of the day, the meaning of the ceremony, the presence of her father, the kindness of the bishop, and the snow. All were like a cluster of beautiful gifts from the Lord.

Just a month later, on February 12, 1889, Louis Martin's condition worsened. He became disoriented and had to be hospitalized at Bon Sauveur, a mental institution in Caen, France. Léonie and Céline boarded at Saint Vincent de Paul orphanage to be near their father and visit him daily. Thérèse and her sisters at Carmel attended to their religious life while feeling the intense pain of their father and two sisters in Caen.

Louis Martin lived at Bon Sauveur for three years. Thérèse took upon herself his suffering and humiliation. As she tidied the refectory (dining room) and swept the corridors, she offered her actions for her father, for priests, for those who suffered in any way. During her stay in Caen, Céline's relationship with the Lord grew, and with that growth came a real desire to follow her sisters to Carmel. Her letters became hymns of confidence in the Lord. When she came to visit Carmel, she and Thérèse shared trusting spiritual conversations. The rest of 1889 passed uneventfully.

Preparing for the Vowed Life

During 1889 Thérèse was a novice. She was given the opportunity to deepen her understanding of the spirituality, the history, and the lifestyle of the Carmelite Order. As a religious she would profess three vows of poverty, chastity, and obedience, according to the spiritual heritage of the Carmelite tradition. Her novice mistress, Sister Marie of the Angels, was particularly gentle. Thérèse's novitiate days, for the most part, were serene. She entrusted her concern for her father to Jesus and poured her energy into spending each day, each moment, doing what she felt the Lord was calling her to do at that specific time.

A few small things could have temporarily caused her to lose her peace of mind. On one occasion, in the evening, during the time of the grand silence, Thérèse filed out of chapel to the closet where the sisters kept their oil lamps. A lamp served as each sister's only source of light, illuminating her small cell until the sunrise the next morning. When Thérèse, at the end of the line, approached the shelf, her lamp was gone. She searched and felt along the edges. The shelf was empty. Thérèse was annoyed at first. It wasn't fair. Each sister had a lamp assigned to her. To take someone else's was unjust. But as Thérèse inched her way along the dark hallway to her room, she began to relax and think about the incident. After all, she reflected, she was preparing herself to take a vow of poverty out of love for Jesus. Poverty, she realized in that moment, could embrace not only the useful things, but even the essential. And if she could find serenity when suffering real inconvenience, she could also find an opportunity to grow. "And so in this *exterior darkness*, I was interiorly illumined," Thérèse explained.[2]

When she had just entered Carmel, Thérèse still preferred pretty things whenever she had the opportunity to have or use them. But as time went on, Thérèse made it a point to choose what was plain or less convenient. She never made any fuss about this, nor did she give an explanation for her unlikely choices. This was the kind of hidden gift, so small in her own estimation, which she could offer to Jesus as an act of love. When someone went into her cell and removed her delicate water jug to replace it with a large chipped one, she smiled and said nothing. Such small spiritual acts were countless. Thérèse liked to offer them for her father, for her family, for priests and religious, for the people who asked for the nuns' prayers, for prisoners. She kept present in her mind all those people in mission lands who still waited to hear the Gospel. Thérèse prayed and performed her duties for missionaries, that they would have the energy, the courage, and the love of God to live their challenging vocation.

As Thérèse prepared water pitchers before meals and put the dining area in order after each meal, she saw the faces of those who were counting on her prayers. She believed that what she did had value in the Church because of the infinite love and mercy of Jesus. She prayed and offered sacrifices for the suffering souls in purgatory as well. The actions of her life were so ordinary, yet she trusted that the infinite love of Jesus could consider the smallest action as a hymn of praise. Even though Thérèse lived inside the walls of a monastery, her love would penetrate the world.

How many times during that novitiate year she must have remembered her pilgrimage to Rome. She could have remembered her train ride through Switzerland: the plush green hills, the valleys and meadows reflecting the bright sun, rippling springs dancing down the hillside, and, in the background, the breathtaking mountains and deep gorges. She remembered the little towns nestled in the mountainsides along the way. Thérèse had sat glued to the window of the train. The passing view had been like a scene out of a picture book and it remained engraved in her memory. She remembered how she had reflected on her vocation to Carmel as the train wound through the mountains.

> I understood how easy it is to become all wrapped up in self, forgetting entirely the sublime goal of one's calling. I said to myself: When I am a prisoner in Carmel and trials come my

way and I have only a tiny bit of the starry heavens to con-
template, I shall remember what my eyes have seen today.
This thought will encourage me and I shall easily forget my
own little interests . . .[3]

Hidden Sacrifices

Thérèse realized how easy it is for people to excuse their
weaknesses and mistakes—as easy as wanting to look good, to
appear virtuous, to be esteemed. Who could be comfortable with
the realization that they were not well thought of by the community? Thérèse's sensitive nature caused her to do battle with
herself. She emphasized hidden simplicity, although her natural
desire to shine posed a constant challenge. Thérèse describes an
example of being misunderstood in *Story of a Soul*. The novice
mistress found a small, broken vase that had fallen from the win-
dowsill. No one had offered any explanation, or even bothered to
pick up the pieces. The novice mistress gathered the pieces of the
vase and approached Thérèse. She showed it to the novice and
admonished her to be more careful. Thérèse's cheeks burned. She
longed to tell the nun that she had not done it. But in that
moment between choices, Thérèse considered. She chose not to
offer an excuse or guess an explanation. Instead, she thanked the
novice mistress, and, as was the custom, she bent low, kissed the
floor, and promised to be more careful in the future.

During her novitiate, Thérèse also spent a good deal of time
attending to the dining area and related duties. Another nun was
also assigned to the task: her sister Pauline. Thérèse was thrilled
to be able to work alongside the sister whom she called her second mother. But the Rule did not permit them to speak to one

another. Thérèse longed to sit for just a little while and pour out her concerns to Pauline, the way she had at *Les Buissonnets*. To forego this consolation was the most difficult sacrifice of all. She had been so free at home. Now she had the gift of her independence to offer the Lord.

On certain occasions Thérèse approached the prioress, Mother de Gonzague, for spiritual direction. Thérèse was thirsty for guidance, being still so new to religious life. However, the prioress spent a significant portion of their hour together scolding her for what seemed to be imperfections. The experience was not pleasant, but Thérèse realized that it was a blessing in its own way. She could not be drawn to any human attachment for the prioress she had known since her childhood.

At the end of Thérèse's novitiate year, Mother de Gonzague told her that her profession of vows would be delayed for another eight months. In her autobiography Thérèse does not elaborate, but her age was most probably the reason for the delay. She would have just turned seventeen. She doesn't say whether or not she anticipated this setback. Rather, her focus was on finding serenity amidst the unexpected and readying herself for profession day.

Profession Day

Eight months passed. Thérèse's profession was set for September 8, 1890. Bishop Hugonin planned to officiate. Céline felt that their father was well enough to travel by carriage from Caen. Though he would not be able to stay for the entire ceremony, Céline thought of how to handle it. She and Louis would arrive toward the end, and he would go up to the grille so that he could give Thérèse his blessing.

The evening before profession found Thérèse in inner turmoil. This was her first bout with temptations about her vocation to religious life, to Carmel. Her life in the monastery flashed before her. The whole thing seemed like a mistake, a ridiculous mistake. She wanted to have a vocation to Carmel, but she probably was not called. By being there she was doing her own will, not God's will—the one thing she feared more than anything. What had she been thinking? How could she have been so blind? She paced the floor of her little cell, trying to find peace. But it was useless. A raging storm replaced the serenity she had so often touched. She couldn't go ahead with the ceremony the next day. She had to get help.

Thérèse sought out her novice mistress and asked to speak with her. The novice's tormented expression spoke more eloquently than words. The novice mistress understood at once what Thérèse was going through. It was a temptation, she assured her. She could go ahead with profession without any more preoccupation. Thérèse felt peace flood her soul again. She went to find the prioress and confided the whole episode to her. As she told her story, Mother de Gonzague laughed softly. She, too, believed that the doubt was only a temptation.

The sky on the morning of September 8 was bright and cloudless. Thérèse was ready to pronounce her vows. Her father was unable to make the trip at all. Deprived of the presence of her earthly father, Thérèse realized she could truly pray the words of the Lord's Prayer: "Our Father who art in heaven." Thérèse pronounced her vows joyfully. Close to her heart she carried a handwritten letter which read:

O Jesus, my Divine Spouse! May I never lose the second robe of my baptism! Take me before I can commit the slightest voluntary fault. May I never see nor find anything but Yourself alone. May creatures be nothing for me, and may I be nothing for them, but may You, Jesus, be *everything*! May the things of earth never be able to trouble my soul, and may nothing disturb my peace. Jesus, I ask You for nothing but peace, and also love, infinite love without any limits other than Yourself; love which is no longer I but You, my Jesus. Jesus, may I die a martyr for You. Give me martyrdom of heart or of body, or rather give me both. Give me grace to fulfill my Vows in all their perfection, and make me understand what a real spouse of Yours should be. Never let me be a burden to the community, let nobody be occupied with me, let me be looked upon as one to be trampled underfoot, forgotten like your little grain of sand, Jesus. May Your will be done in me perfectly, and may I arrive at the place you have prepared for me.

Jesus, allow me to save very many souls; let no soul be lost today; let all the souls in purgatory be saved. Jesus, pardon me if I say anything I should not say. I want only to give You joy and to console You.[4]

The ceremony in which Thérèse would receive the veil was set for September 24, 1890. Thérèse looked forward with delight to having Bishop Hugonin and her father there. But neither could come. Bishop Hugonin was ill and her father was too weak to travel. Humanly speaking, it was a sad day for Thérèse. She cried and noted how her tears were misunderstood. Still, Jesus had permitted this. He left her without special graces on that day. Without his help, she admitted, she could do nothing but cry.

Chapter Twelve

Strength to Soar

From October 8 through October 15, 1891, Father Alexis Prou, a Franciscan from Caen, preached an annual retreat to the nuns of the Lisieux Carmel. Thérèse made a novena to prepare herself well. She did not always find preached retreats practical for her particular life situation. Besides, she had heard that Father Alexis' "specialty" was reconciling great sinners with the Church. After the retreat master had spoken just a few words, Thérèse received the grace to understand that the Lord himself had provided this priest as the guide for this retreat to help her to grow in the spiritual life. Thérèse felt that Father Alexis understood her. She wrote later:

> He launched me full sail upon the waves of *confidence and love* which so strongly attracted me, but upon which I dared not advance.[1]

The other sisters did not draw the same insights from the retreat homilies. Thérèse was convinced that the Lord had given her a singular invitation to proceed on the way of love. In fact, she was the only one who truly appreciated that retreat. Thérèse deepened her penetration of the power of love as a means to progress rapidly in the spiritual life. She realized initially that love alone had the capacity to help her overcome her natural fears and timidity. Love gave her the strength to soar.

Mother Genevieve's Legacy

Thérèse continued to hear God speaking to her through the words of others. Mother Genevieve was another source of inspiration for Thérèse. She so admired the elderly nun propped up in the infirmary bed. Mother Genevieve had become holy, Thérèse felt, by practicing hidden, ordinary virtues. Thérèse stopped in her room one day, intending to stay only a moment because two sisters were already visiting. The Rule permitted only two at a time. As the young sister backed away, Mother Genevieve offered her a thought: "Serve God with *peace and joy*; remember, my child, *our God is a God of peace*."[2] Thérèse had been having a difficult day and Mother Genevieve's words lifted her spirits immediately.

On the following Sunday, Thérèse went again to the infirmary to visit. Thérèse had thought about Mother's wise advice during that week and asked if what she had said had been a revelation. The old nun assured Thérèse that the message had come from her, not from any extraordinary intervention.

Thérèse remembered how she had gone to visit Mother Genevieve on her profession day. The young sister had manifested the terrible temptation she had done battle with the night before she had pronounced her vows. Mother Genevieve explained that she had also gone through a similar trial before professing her vows.

Thérèse was one of the sisters who assisted Mother Genevieve during her final hours on this earth. On December 5, 1891, the elderly nun was near death. Thérèse stood at the foot of the bed, facing Mother. A kind of numbness took over as Thérèse watched and prayed. Time ticked slowly by. Just before Mother Genevieve passed into eternity, Thérèse experienced joy filling her whole being. She felt fervent, encouraged in her vocation. Thérèse remembered at that moment that once she had told Mother Genevieve that she would never see purgatory. Mother had replied simply that she hoped not.

After her death, the sisters prayed and mourned in silence at her bedside. Then each slipped away. Several took some small token of remembrance, some small relic. Thérèse's relic was unique. When Mother Genevieve was laid out in the choir, Thérèse waited until no one was around. She moved closer and, taking a small piece of linen cloth, she collected one lone tear that still glistened on the dead nun's eyelid. That tear was for Thérèse, and she felt that it was a tear of joy. Soon after, Thérèse had a dream. The elderly nun was making out her will and dispensing her treasures to the community of sisters gathered around her. Thérèse, being one of the youngest, was last. She felt preoccupied because Mother Genevieve would have nothing left to give her. But the dream led to a wonderful surprise. Thérèse stood in front of Mother Genevieve, who smiled at her and said three times: "To you I leave my heart."[3] When Thérèse woke up, she remembered the incident vividly.

Influenza at Carmel

On Thérèse's nineteenth birthday, Sister St. Joseph, the oldest member of the community, died. It was January 2, 1892. Two other sisters also died: Sister Magdalene and Sister Febronie, the mother subprioress. Thérèse found Sister Magdalene dead in her cell. She hastened to the sacristy and returned to place a wreath of roses on Sister Magdalene's head. Then Thérèse sought help. As the influenza worked its course, Thérèse and two others were the only nuns still standing. They served the community and tried to take care of each sister's needs. Sister St. Stanislaus, the head sacristan, was also in bed and was very ill. Thérèse took care of the sacristy and arranged all of the details for the funerals. Thérèse wrote, "It's impossible to imagine the sad state of the community at this time . . ."[4] Yet, she was able to find reason to be joyful even in the midst of that trial. Through it all, she was given permission to receive Communion every day. She was also pleased to be able, as temporary sacristan, to touch and care for the sacred vessels used by the priest for the celebration of Mass.

Despite the consolations, Thérèse often felt drowsy and distracted during prayer times. After Communion, as she struggled to pray with fervor, Thérèse resolved to continue her thanksgiving throughout her day. One morning she wondered if the Lord could possibly be pleased with her. She asked for a little sign. If he was upset, would he let the priest give her just half a host at communion time? Thérèse's turn came to receive the Holy Eucharist. She watched as the priest took two hosts and placed them reverently on her tongue.

Pauline: My Living Jesus

God continued to fill Thérèse's life with surprise. On February 20, 1893, Sister Agnes of Jesus (Thérèse's second oldest sister Pauline) was elected prioress of the Lisieux Carmel. She was appointed for a three-year term. Five years after Thérèse's death, on April 19, 1902, Mother Agnes was again elected prioress. In 1923, Pope Pius XI, who beatified and canonized Thérèse, confirmed Mother Agnes as prioress of the Lisieux Carmel for life. She died on July 28, 1951, at the age of ninety.

Thérèse was overjoyed that Pauline was appointed prioress, but she was subdued in her jubilation, out of sensitivity for the feelings and preferences of the others. The youngest of the Martins looked up to Pauline and learned to read the book of Jesus in her life. Thérèse understood her sister's sensitive heart and saw the inevitable daily crosses and contradictions Pauline endured. Thérèse noted the tranquility of her older sister, a tranquility she recognized to be the fruit of suffering accepted for love of Jesus. It was the Lord himself who had unfolded the mysteriously charming quality of suffering to the little queen. Her memory flashed back to the boarding school where she had fumbled along to mingle with her peers. Who had understood her there in the early adolescent years? Only Jesus, who waited for her in the silence of the tabernacle. And she had felt accepted by him, drawn to his heart, confident that he loved her. It was like her father's love stretched to the infinite. Now, thinking back to the loneliness and pain, Thérèse reflected that these tools brought her closer to Jesus. The very same tools were at work in Pauline's life to make her religious life rich and fruitful, not only for her, but for the people who counted on her prayers and sacrificial life-style. "Very truly, I tell you, unless a grain of wheat falls into the earth and dies, it remains just a single grain; but if it dies, it bears much fruit" (Jn 12:24).

As Thérèse continued her day-to-day life at Carmel, she reflected on her desires and motivations. She was in awe of Pauline's talents for painting and composing poetry. Thérèse saw these talents offered to Jesus for his glory as something wonder-ful. She thought of how pleasing they must be to the Lord. Although she felt strongly drawn to pursue painting or the writ-ing of poetry herself, she would never ask permission to follow the inclination. Why should she seek good things unless the Lord wanted them for her? She reflected on the words of Ecclesiastes: "Then I considered all that my hands had done and the toil I had spent in doing it, and again, all was vanity and a chasing after wind, and there was nothing to be gained under the sun" (Eccl 2:11).

Thérèse was astonished when she too was given the opportu-nity to develop her talents for painting and writing poetry, but she was at peace about it as well because she had not asked or manifested her desire for these. It was the Lord's gift to her because she had tried to remain humble. She also learned that gifts and talents do not take one away from God unless one for-gets the source of the gifts. When the receiver recognizes the divine Giver, the very recognition serves to draw that person closer to God.

The Best for My King

As Thérèse grew closer to her Heavenly Father, she continued to pray for her beloved earthly father. From the date he was released from Bon Sauveur in 1892, until his death two years later, Louis Martin visited Carmel only once. Céline and Isidore Guerin helped the frail, old man as he stepped into the monastery entrance. How familiar this building was to him. When Louis was leaving he looked upward for a long time and said aloud with feeling: "In heaven." Thérèse gazed at her father until his figure had burned itself into her memory. She would never forget the details of this visit, which was to be her father's last. Louis Martin died on July 29, 1894. He was seventy years old.

Louis Martin's death and Céline's entrance into Carmel are closely linked. A few months after her father's death, Céline became the fourth Martin sister to join the Carmel of Lisieux. It was September 14, 1894. Thérèse and her sisters were jubilant.

From the day Thérèse had entered Carmel, April 9, 1888, until Céline actually entered the Order, Thérèse had prayed for her sister. Thérèse suffered to think of the temptations that the world threw at her. Céline, considered by Thérèse as "my other self," was especially precious to her. Although Thérèse could have accepted and respected Céline's decision to choose another calling or another Order, she was convinced that Céline's place was at Carmel. This was her prayer, her hope that she took to the feet of her Spouse.

There were obstacles of course. When the community was consulted about the possibility of accepting Céline into the Order, one of the senior members, Sister Aimee of Jesus, objected strenuously. She felt that three sisters from the same family was sufficient for a community of about twenty nuns. Sister Aimee of Jesus was convinced and there seemed no changing her mind.

Thérèse was praying her thanksgiving after Communion one morning. She had two particular intentions: could the Lord in his goodness convince Sister Aimee to reverse her decision, thus removing the obstacle to Céline's entrance into Carmel? The second: would the Lord do this wonderful thing as a sign that her father was in heaven with God? With childlike trust, Thérèse prayed and believed that she would receive a sign. She wanted to know that her father was not in purgatory, but enjoying eternal bliss. After all, at her request the Lord had moved the hardened sinner, Henri Pranzini, to repentance moments before his execution; Thérèse also had been given snow the morning she received her religious habit. She had even been able to find her favorite wildflower, the corn cockle, in the garden of Carmel. If Jesus was willing to take care of major and minor details in her life to please his beloved, wouldn't he take care of these most important matters: her father's eternal happiness and Céline's vocation? Yes, Thérèse believed he would. She rose and left the choir.

Someone was waiting in the shadows. Thérèse was startled for a moment, but then quickly identified the figure. It was Sister Aimee of Jesus. Thérèse managed a feeble smile. "Could we speak for a moment?" the older nun asked, pointing to a nearby room. Tears filled Sister Aimee's eyes as she struggled to find the words. At last she said softly, "I have changed my mind about my opposition to Céline's entrance into Carmel." Thérèse was ecstatic.[5] This was better than snow, better than her favorite flower. This pertained to the most precious gifts of life: salvation and sanctification. Together, Sister Aimee and Sister Thérèse went to tell Mother Agnes of Jesus the wonderful news. Thérèse recognized with gratitude the graces the Lord was granting her. She was at peace about her father and Céline.

Céline, the object of so many prayers, entered Carmel September of 1894. She was given the name Sister Genevieve of the Holy Face.

Love Alone Attracts Me

The joy of Céline's entrance gave Thérèse an opportunity to reflect on the Lord's goodness to her. She could see herself being directed by Jesus in her spiritual life. Other attractions, such as the desire to suffer and to die for Jesus, had lost their appeal. Thérèse was led to understand that the most important treasure of all is love and the way to obtain it is abandonment to God in everything. She wrote:

> Now, abandonment alone guides me. I have no other compass! I can no longer ask for anything with fervor except the accomplishment of God's will in my soul.[6]

In the first years after she entered Carmel, Thérèse read and found comfort in the mystical writings of the Carmelite doctor of the Church, Saint John of the Cross. But as time went on she drifted away from reading even the best of books. At this time, she focused her meditations and spiritual reading on two books only: the Bible and *The Imitation of Christ*. She felt drawn to these books alone. She became convinced that Jesus was working in her soul without words. She felt that he was there throughout her day, enlightening her to understand and grasp situations, to choose wisely, to say and do what was right. From experience she realized that God's kingdom was within her.

Thérèse felt irresistibly attracted by the infinite mercy of God. She realized that the Lord was offering her many graces, which convinced her that God should be loved, not feared. She saw love as the purifier and motivation for weak human beings. She felt that through love, "no one would ever consent to cause Him any pain."[7] Thérèse saw all of God's perfection—even his justice—as rooted in love. On June 9, 1895, while at Mass, Thérèse received the inspiration to offer herself to Merciful Love. Two days later, with the permission of Mother Agnes of Jesus, the prioress, Thérèse and Céline together made the *Act of Oblation to Merciful Love*.

Finding Jesus' Face in Daily Trials

Céline's arrival at the monastery provided Thérèse some solace and joy, but she also continued to embrace the hardships of life in Carmel. Céline's testimony at the Church's investigation into the holiness of Thérèse commented on the virtues Thérèse practiced in a heroic way.

Céline testified how she had confided to her sister that she found it difficult to be equally kind to all the sisters in community. Thérèse took the time to explain to Céline the importance of not showing preferences. In fact, Thérèse drew on an example from her own life. She mentioned by name a sister who was particularly annoying to her. Céline was astounded. She had seen Thérèse interacting with this sister. Thérèse was so kind and sensitive that Céline believed that this particular sister was one of Thérèse's closest friends. These small but heroic acts were what set Thérèse on a little way to sainthood.

CHAPTER THIRTEEN

Challenges to Love

Thérèse considered her spiritual life with utter seriousness and thought frequently about what was really important in life. She observed the human tendency of being attached to the things of this earth. How easy it is, she admitted, to become distracted by the delights of this life and to forget God, the Source of all good. Of course, it was easier, as a cloistered religious for Thérèse to be more detached from the things of this earth. She possessed less and she saw less. She had chosen this way of life as an act of love for Jesus.

But she wisely realized that even a nun could find ways to be attached to her own preferences. Thérèse wrote of concrete examples, such as the time ideas she had shared during recreation or in conversation with a sister were plagiarized by others. Something inside her naturally rebelled at the injustice. Yet if she were truly poor as her vow of poverty challenged her to be, she could not claim anything as her own, not even her clever ideas. Thérèse examined her heart on her relationships in community. She tried to honestly verify whether she was courageously striving to remove any spirit of competition. To guard against human tendencies that could block the work of the Holy Spirit in her, Thérèse deliberately chose to go against her preferences and inclinations. At community recreations, the sisters would enjoy each others' company. Some nuns were much more approachable and interesting. Thérèse would rarely seek them out. They had plenty of affection. She, instead, would focus her attention on those who were more withdrawn or harder to please.

Thérèse saw herself as an artist's little brush to be used for the finishing touches on a canvas. Thérèse confided that the first time she, the little brush, was used by the Lord was in her postulancy, when she and another young woman, Martha, were the two postulants. Although Martha was eight years older than Thérèse, the two quickly became good friends. The two friends were permitted to have spiritual conversations. At first, this was very enlightening to Thérèse. But as time passed, she noticed that things were changing. Their chats were becoming less spiritual. Although younger, Thérèse felt it was her responsibility to speak up and suggest to her friend that the conversations be elevated to a spiritual plane. She also helped Martha to become aware of the challenge to overcome natural attachments to some sisters, even the prioress. It was necessary to keep one's heart rooted in the love of Jesus. Thérèse's friend was embarrassed at first, but then, on reflection, Martha admitted the wisdom of Thérèse's advice and followed it. The two became even better friends in the true spirit of Carmel.

Thérèse battled her affectionate nature and overcame the desire to make excuses that would bring her into contact and conversation with her two older sisters. She longed for the crumbs of human consolation, even just a word or a smile from Pauline and Marie. But the halls of Carmel were silent and empty.

After her profession of vows, Thérèse continued to choose the more difficult path. She asked for and received permission to remain in the novitiate, where the atmosphere was stricter. From 1893 to 1896, she was asked to look after her novitiate companions, helping them adjust to monastic life. In March, 1896, she became the acting novice mistress—although she never formally held the title—a duty she carried out until May of 1897.

Thérèse's own sister Céline became one of her novices. Céline admired her youngest sister's mature, sensitive manner and the ways in which Thérèse made herself available and helpful to the young women. Thérèse sought to better know the novices and to guide and lead these "lambs of Jesus" to green pastures. With some novices she would be gentle, admitting how hard it was for her as well in a particular situation or in the practice of a certain virtue. With other novices, Thérèse would be straightforward, almost blunt. She realized that she could not employ the gentle approach with sisters who could have seen admissions of struggle as weaknesses of character. "I know very well that your little lambs find me severe," [1] she lamented to Jesus. Because Thérèse was not officially the novice mistress, some novices were rude and occasionally insulting to the young sister who went against their grain.

Other novices, however, were a delight. Thérèse tells of one who was her special charge. This sister had come from another

Carmel. Her name was Sister Marie of the Trinity. One morning, at the beginning of Lent, 1895, Sister Marie approached Thérèse, her face radiant. She recounted her dream of the night before. Sister Thérèse listened intently. In her dream, Sister Marie was talking to her own sister, a young woman who was very attracted to worldly living. The Carmelite was explaining stanza thirteen of a poem Sister Thérèse had recently written, entitled "Living on Love." The particular words in the dream were:

"Loving you, Jesus, is such a fruitful loss! . . .
All my perfumes are yours forever."[2]

When Sister Marie awoke, the memory of the dream remained. Was it a sign that her sister might become a nun? Was it an invitation to Sister Marie to write to her sister suggesting that she consider the possibility of a religious vocation? Could she write to her sister as soon as Lent was over? Thérèse very kindly encouraged her to do so, but told her to first ask the prioress, Mother Agnes (Pauline), which was the custom. No doubt Thérèse did not expect the reply Sister Marie received. Because Lent was still far from being over, Mother Agnes did not consider letter writing a priority, even for such a worthy cause as encouraging a possible religious vocation. Mother responded that Carmelites saved souls not through letters, but through prayer.

Thérèse interpreted this answer as the Lord's desire that she and Sister Marie of the Trinity pray for the young woman. They prayed ardently for the rest of Lent. As the feast of the resurrection brought renewed joy and hope, Sister Marie of the Trinity's sister did enter religious life and consecrated herself to Jesus.

Sister Thérèse called this a miracle, attributed to the prayers of a believing novice who was humble enough to trust.

Sister St. Pierre

Thérèse's attention was not only focused on the younger novices. She also was very attentive to the needs of the elderly sisters, especially one in particular named Sister St. Pierre.

Pain was as familiar to Sister St. Pierre as her Carmelite calling. During the time when Thérèse was a novice, Sister St. Pierre was still able to maneuver her arthritic body to the choir and the refectory. During evening prayer before supper, she was directly in front of Thérèse. The novice had never experienced the kind of joint pain that plagued Sister St. Pierre, but she knew that the elderly nun was suffering. At ten minutes to six each evening, Sister St. Pierre would shake her hourglass, signaling that it was time for her to begin her slow, careful walk to the community dining room. Someone would have to assist her to steady her steps. It was a volunteer situation, and Thérèse wanted to be of service.

The old nun looked cautiously into the face of the young novice. What if Thérèse could not do it? What if she hurried or went too slow? What if she should fall? In the beginning, Thérèse experienced reluctance, even dread as the time approached. She knew she could never please the nun. It would be so easy to step back and let others try. They might be more capable, successful. But Thérèse went back with astounding regularity. She not only learned Sister St. Pierre's routine, she mastered it. Down the hall they went, making their way to the nun's seat in the dining room.

Thérèse then folded Sister St. Pierre's sleeves back, careful not to hurt the twisted, swollen hands. That was all that was required, but Thérèse realized that it was very hard for Sister St. Pierre to cut her bread. So Thérèse added this simple service. The elderly nun was completely won over.

One evening as they walked down the dimly lit corridor, Thérèse heard joyful music drifting through the cloister walls. She knew there must have been an elegant supper party going on in one of the nearby villas. Her imagination painted the bright rooms, plush furniture, a banquet, and happy guests. She understood that this was not her life. Nor would it ever be. She looked into the face of Sister St. Pierre, and then glanced around at the stark brick walls. How beautiful they seemed to her! She was where she belonged.

When Thérèse wrote her *Story of a Soul*, she recalled that she considered her daily walks with Sister St. Pierre a splendid opportunity to find Jesus in her suffering sister.

Thérèse also discovered a multitude of other little ways to learn patience in Carmel. Once, she was assigned a seat in choir near a nun who made a strange little noise as she prayed and meditated. Thérèse described it as two seashells being scraped together. Instead of letting the tension mount in her, Thérèse listened attentively and imagined that the irritating noise was really a lovely concert. In fact, it became a concert because Thérèse offered the sound to Jesus, trusting that he could turn it into a symphony. In the living of her ordinary daily life, Thérèse found the verses for her hymn of love.

Chapter Fourteen

Embracing the Cross

On Saturday, March 21, 1896, the day before Passion Sunday, the Carmelites of Lisieux held their election for prioress. Sixteen of the sisters voted; the other eight prayed for the outcome according to God's will. Thérèse was among the eight who waited and prayed. When the election was final, the bell was rung and the entire community gathered in choir. Thérèse entered. The first thing she saw was Mother Marie de Gonzague in the prioress's chair.

Humanly speaking, it must have been a deep disappointment that her sister, Mother Agnes, had not been elected for another term. But Thérèse recognized the opportunity to trust in God and to see the prioress as the representative of Jesus. The momentary jolt she experienced subsided, and her little boat continued on its tranquil course. Thérèse's poetry sings the secrets of her soul and the reason for her serenity. Verse four of "Living on Love," dated February 26, 1895, explains:

> Living on Love is not setting up one's tent
> At the top of Tabor.
> It's climbing Calvary with Jesus,
> It's looking at the cross as a treasure! . . .
> In heaven I'm to live on joy.
> Then trials will have fled forever,
> But in exile, in suffering I want
> To live on Love.[1]

Discovery on Good Friday

Thérèse did not fear the cross. She wanted to share the sufferings of her Spouse. With this disposition she had embraced the austere Carmelite Lenten fast with her usual youthful enthusiasm. The nuns remained in adoration before the Blessed Sacrament on the night between Holy Thursday and Good Friday. Thérèse had not obtained permission to do so and went to her room at midnight. She put out her oil lamp and retired. Just as her head rested on the pillow, Thérèse felt her mouth fill with warm fluid. She groped for her handkerchief and brought it to her lips. Could it be blood? Her first impulse was to check the handkerchief, but she had already extinguished her light. She decided to offer up the sacrifice of her curiosity to Jesus for someone in need. She would examine her handkerchief in the morning.

When the bell sounded the time for rising the next morning, Thérèse drew back her window shutters and peered down at her handkerchief. It was stained with blood. She sought out Mother Marie de Gonzague to tell her. But Thérèse emphasized how well she felt and how much she wanted to continue the Lenten austerities. Mother clearly did not grasp the seriousness of Thérèse's condition and she consented. During the work periods that day, Thérèse cleaned the windows of the doors, helping to prepare the convent for the glory of Easter. During the evening of April 3, 1896, Thérèse had her second hemoptysis or hemorrhage. This was a sign of the likely presence of tuberculosis, a contagious disease of the lungs. In Thérèse's day, the medical profession offered home remedies to alleviate the patient's suffering, but there was no known cure.

Thérèse was aware that she was probably dying, but her main preoccupation centered on her desire to reach heaven. In the meantime, she wanted to carry out her community duties without interruption for as long as possible. That included the austere penitential prayers and practices. She did not want to be exempted from any of the rigors called for in daily convent life. She saw fidelity to her duty and volunteering for extra assignments as her little way to Jesus. This was her hymn of love, not a glorious, magnificent hymn of the martyrs and doctors of the Church, but a small, constant hymn, awesome in its totality. On Easter Sunday, April 5, 1896, Thérèse felt the joy of her risen Lord and harbored in her heart the realization that she would soon enough be with her Spouse forever.

From Good Friday 1896 until her death on September 30, 1897, Thérèse walked the road to Calvary. Because her painful yet faithful journey is recorded in her own *Story of a Soul* and the *Her Last Conversations* carefully written down by Mother

Agnes, anyone who cares to can approach her bedside and witness a saga of faith. While Thérèse celebrated the joy of Easter 1896, the Lord soon after permitted her to be afflicted with a piercing gloom, a dark night in which she was tormented by doubts against faith. It seemed to her that heaven was a mirage, a fantasy. Beyond the grave was nothing. Thérèse pictured the still body of her mother. She recalled how as a child of four she had kissed her mother's cold cheek. Where was her mother? Where was her father? They were with God in heaven; she knew it. She believed it. She mustered every bit of energy to affirm her belief in God, in Jesus, in the Creed, in eternal life. And even if she couldn't see or have anything at all to cling to in this life, she would never abandon the Lord. No matter how dark it seemed to be with him at this time, to reject him would be the greatest tragedy. Thérèse's face was serene. The anxiety of her soul was never exteriorly manifested as she quietly continued to follow the monastic schedule. She was the assistant novice mistress during this period, and would remain such until that May. The novices never guessed, never even suspected, Thérèse's inner turmoil—a torment that would continue up until a few moments before her birth to new life.

Help From Heaven

Thérèse responded to her illness with strength and composure, but her inner turmoil caused her great anguish. In *Story of a Soul*, Thérèse describes a heavenly consolation she received that was the cause of joy for her in this difficult time. She had a dream in which she saw three nuns walking toward her. They were dressed in the distinctive Carmelite garb, mantles and long veils. She remembers that in her dream she longed to see the face of at least one of the Carmelites. As if in answer to her request, the tall sister in the middle lifted the veil that fell over her face and covered Thérèse with it.

Thérèse knelt and felt overwhelmed with joy as she looked up into the face of Venerable Anne of Jesus. Thérèse recognized her as the foundress of the Carmelite Order in France. Mother Anne smiled at Thérèse with a heart filled with love. Because Venerable Anne was so approachable, Thérèse asked her with confidence if she would remain a long time on this earth or be with Jesus in heaven soon. The answer was soon. Thérèse then asked if Jesus was pleased with her or if she should be doing something more for his glory. Mother Anne assured Thérèse that the Lord was contented with her. Just as she started to ask about her sisters, Thérèse woke up, but the joy lingered on.

Called to Be Love

Thérèse's impending death led her to think about the life she had led since she entered Carmel. Six years had passed since she had made her profession of vows, years of rapid spiritual development and growth. Thérèse had a great heart. She wanted to respond to the Lord with her own small love in thanksgiving for the love he had extended to her. Her grateful prayer led her to desire to thank him by living out all the vocations in the Church. She wanted to be an apostle, a priest, a missionary, a martyr, a prophet, a doctor, whatever would bring the love of Jesus—that same love that had touched her life—to all people. She realized that she was undeserving of the faith and of her Carmelite vocation. Nothing that she could do or say could merit those gifts that were beyond her capacity to acquire for herself. It was Love that had gifted her. It was infinite Love that gave value to every ministry in the Church.

With her characteristic enthusiasm, Thérèse's imagination was hard at work. She saw the walls of her Carmelite convent come down brick by brick. Before the eyes of her soul lay the whole world. With Saint Paul, she wanted to be all to all. The great apostle had described the Christian meaning of love. Thérèse understood what Paul wrote.

> I understood that LOVE COMPRISED ALL VOCA-
> TIONS, THAT LOVE WAS EVERYTHING, THAT IT
> EMBRACED ALL TIMES AND PLACES. . . . IN A
> WORD, THAT IT WAS ETERNAL!
>
> Then, in the excess of my delirious joy, I cried out: O
> Jesus, my Love . . . my *vocation*, at last I have found it. . . . MY
> VOCATION IS LOVE!
>
> Yes, I have found my place in the Church and it is You,
> O my God, who have given me this place; in the heart of the
> Church, my Mother, I shall be *Love*. Thus I shall be every-
> thing, and thus my dream will be realized.[2]

Chapter Fifteen

On the Road to Calvary

Thérèse's health declined steadily. Her youthful energy was ebbing away. She poured all her strength into the performance of her daily tasks, but eventually she could no longer go on. Still she pushed her pen across the page of her copybook to record her spiritual journey, as her superiors had asked of her.

She wrote:

> [E]ver since I got sick, the cares you [Mother Marie de Gonzague] bestowed on me taught me a great deal about charity. No remedy appeared too expensive to you, and when it did not succeed you tried another thing without tiring. When I was going to recreation, what attention you paid in order to shelter me from drafts! Finally, if I wanted to tell all, I would never end.
>
> When thinking over all these things, I told myself that I should be as compassionate toward the spiritual infirmities of my Sisters as you are, dear Mother, when caring for me with so much love.[1]

Thérèse reflected on various phrases of Scripture. She considered the anxiety of Martha when Jesus visited her and her sister at Bethany. "It is not Martha's works that Jesus finds fault with. . . . It is only the *restlessness* of His ardent hostess that He willed to correct."[2] She managed a few more paragraphs as she pushed her pencil doggedly ahead. The last words she recorded in her copybook were:

> Yes, I feel it; even though I had on my conscience all the sins that can be committed, I would go, my heart broken with sorrow, and throw myself into Jesus' arms, for I know how much He loves the prodigal child who returns to Him. It is not because God, in His anticipating mercy, has preserved my soul from mortal sin that I go to him with confidence and love."[3]

In June of 1897 Thérèse was relieved of her convent duties. Her only remaining assignment was to complete the writing of her autobiography. She worked on it until July, spending much of her time outdoors in the garden in order to take advantage of the fresh air and sunshine. July 6 marked the beginning of a new stage in her illness. She began again to periodically vomit blood. This continued until August 5. On July 8, Thérèse was moved to the monastery infirmary where she would spend the remainder of her life. On that same day the statue of Mary, the Virgin of the Smile, was brought to her room. Thérèse could clearly see its serene face, and she remembered vividly that Mary, in this very statue, had smiled at her when she was just ten years old. That smile of her heavenly mother had healed her.

The infirmary had a bed surrounded by curtains and a comfortable chair that she could sit in when she felt well enough.

Thérèse pinned to the bed curtains her favorite holy pictures: "the Holy Face of Christ, the Blessed Virgin, her 'dear little' Theophane Venard, etc."[4] Theophane Venard had been a young, French, missionary priest born in 1829. He had died a martyr in Hanoi, Indochina (now Vietnam). He was declared blessed by Pope Pius X on May 2, 1909, twelve years after the death of Thérèse, and was among a group, the Martyrs of Vietnam, who were declared saints by Pope John Paul II. Thérèse was deeply inspired by Father Venard. She mentioned him often during the final stages of her illness.

Doctor de Corniere, the community's physician, stressed the seriousness of Thérèse's condition. The young nun was racked with pain. Headaches and a piercing pain in her side tormented her. Frequently she felt she was suffocating and gasped frantically for air as the sweltering summer days bathed the small infirmary in humidity. The sisters adjusted her pillows and moved her gently in an effort to make her more comfortable. But there was little relief.

During the month of July, Thérèse had some intervals when she felt stronger. She manifested a cheerfulness that amazed the nuns who cared for her. The Anointing of the Sick was postponed because she did not seem sick enough. (In Thérèse's time, the Anointing of the Sick, called Extreme Unction, was administered only when a person was in imminent danger of death.) She was still able to carry on brief conversations with Mother Agnes (Pauline) and could answer her questions and the questions of her other two sisters, Marie and Céline. Thérèse agreed that after her death some of her remembrances could be used for the information circular that would be sent to other Carmelite monasteries. Gradually, cautiously, her sisters spoke about the eventual publication of her memoirs for everyone who wanted to read them. Thérèse did not oppose the idea, but she immediately entrusted the project to Mother Agnes. Of her autobiography, Thérèse said: "There will be something in it for all tastes, except for those in extraordinary ways."[5]

In the days that followed, Thérèse articulated her vocation to love from heaven. She said to her sister Pauline, "How unhappy I shall be in heaven if I cannot do little favors on earth for those whom I love . . . I will return! I shall come down!"[6] On July 17, 1897, Thérèse voiced the prediction that was to become not only famous but also a marvelous source of consolation to countless people:

> I especially feel that my mission is about to begin, my mission of making God loved as I love Him, of giving my little way to souls. If God answers my desires, my heaven will be spent on earth until the end of the world. Yes, I want to spend my heaven in doing good on earth.[7]

On July 28, Thérèse's condition worsened. She endured an attack that she described as the beginning of "great sufferings." Doctor de Corniere announced that she would not live through the night. Quietly the sisters prepared an adjacent room with the things that would be needed for her burial. She received Holy Communion and the Anointing of the Sick.

The long night of July 28 quietly led into the dawn of July 29. As light slid through the window to announce another sultry day, Thérèse opened her eyes. She had survived the crisis. Thérèse was serene. The previous day she had expected to die. Now the doctor told her she had about a month to live. She said to Mother Agnes:

"What does it matter if I remain a long time on earth? If I suffer very much and always more, I will not fear, for God will give me strength; he'll never abandon me."[8]

Thérèse ceased coughing up blood on August 5 and enjoyed two weeks of calm. Doctor de Corniere was confident enough of her stability that he went on vacation.

Unpredictably a new attack began on August 15. Thérèse suffered coughing spells, difficulty in breathing, chest pains, and swollen limbs. The nearest available doctor was Thérèse's cousin through marriage, Doctor Francis La Neele. He rushed from Caen when the Carmelites of Lisieux called him. Doctor La Neele was the first to identify Thérèse's illness as tuberculosis. He reported that she was breathing with only half a lung and that the disease was now attacking her intestines. Thérèse's pain was unbearable. She described it as being stretched out on "iron spikes." When told of the doctor's fear that gangrene was setting in, Thérèse replied: "Well, all the better! While I am at it I may as well suffer very much and all over—and even have several sicknesses at the same time!"[9]

As she lay in pain, she apologized for crying out in agony. "What a grace it is to have faith! If I had no faith, I would have inflicted death on myself without hesitating a moment!"[10]

Thérèse experienced another period of peace lasting from the end of August until September 13. During this time, she was cheerful and serene. She delighted the sisters who stopped by briefly to see her. She even teased about the doctor's inability to help. But she knew that despite this peaceful interlude, death was near. She told Mother Agnes that she trusted "Papa God." She thanked the sisters, including her own blood sisters, who were so devoted to her. She personified a hymn of gratitude. As she lay dying, offering her sufferings for everyone throughout the world, she fulfilled her own words: "Jesus does not demand great actions from us but simply *surrender* and *gratitude*."[11]

Thérèse received Communion for the last time on August 19. She offered that Communion for a former Carmelite priest, Father Hyacinthe Loyson. Her prayers, her sufferings, her darkness, her perplexities were offered in the chalice of the Church for the good of others. "Everything I have, everything I merit is for the Church and for souls."[12]

Thérèse's bed had been moved to the center of the infirmary. From there she could look out of the window and enjoy the sight of the cloister garden. It was like a patch of *Les Buissonnets*. What beautiful memories she held of her father and her sisters. She would see her father and her mother very soon. They were only days apart. Thérèse's aunt and uncle, Isidore and Céline Guerin, sent little treats, even a chocolate éclair, to please her. On August 30, Thérèse's bed was rolled to the entrance of the choir so she could see it for the last time. Her sister Céline, (now Sister Genevieve), photographed her there. In this last photo, Thérèse is holding a crucifix, trying, painfully, to smile. September 8, 1897, was the seventh anniversary of her religious profession. The sisters decorated her room with a sea of flowers. Thérèse was moved at their thoughtfulness. She wanted to share her gift with the Virgin of the Smile. With great care, she wove a garland of flowers, and the sisters draped it around Our Lady's neck.

Doctor de Corniere returned from vacation to find Thérèse in critical condition. Her remaining lung, also infected with tuberculosis, made the effort to breath nearly unbearable. She was suffocating and spoke in short raspy sentences. "Mama," she said to Mother Agnes, "earth's air is denied to me, when will God grant me the air of heaven?"[13] Thérèse's body was crucified, her emotions were shrouded in gloom; she was exhausted beyond the remedy of sleep. The night was with her all the time. The feeling of emptiness led her to the border of despair. She chased the desperate thoughts from her mind. She would not give in to them. She gasped: "It is into God's arms that I'm falling."[14]

The days of September crept by. On September 29, Thérèse's breathing grew even more labored. After Doctor de Corniere's visit, she asked Mother de Gonzague: "Is it today, Mother?" The prioress answered softly: "Yes, my child."[15] Thérèse lingered the rest of that day and one more painful night. She received the sacrament of Reconciliation and then waited peacefully for her Lord to come for her. Sister Genevieve of the Holy Face and Sister Marie of the Sacred Heart remained at Thérèse's side during the night. Mother Agnes of Jesus joined them in the morning.

On September 30, Thérèse's condition grew worse. Around 3:00 P.M. she extended her arms in the shape of a cross. She rested one arm on Mother Agnes's shoulder, and the other on Sister Genevieve's. She wanted to be a victim of love as was her Savior. The Lord was soon to grant her the death of love for which she prayed. At about 4:30 in the afternoon, Mother Agnes was alone with Thérèse and became alarmed when all the color drained rapidly from her sister's face. Mother de Gonzague and the entire community returned. Thérèse smiled, but remained silent. During the next two hours the death rattle shook her. Thérèse's "face was flushed, her hands purple, and her feet were as cold as ice."[16] Even while she shivered, beads of perspiration covered her forehead and cheeks. She smiled at Sister Genevieve who bathed her parched lips with ice.

The Angelus bell rang at 6:00 P.M. Thérèse gazed at the statue of the Virgin of the Smile. She clutched her crucifix. The infirmary was tranquil. The sisters, who had been there with her for two hours, quietly slipped away. Thérèse spoke briefly with Mother de Gonzague. Then she rested her head on the pillow, turning her face toward the right. The prioress acted quickly. She had the monastery bell rung, summoning the nuns back to the room. As the community knelt, Thérèse, her eyes riveted to her crucifix, exclaimed: "Oh! I love Him! . . . My God! . . . I love You!"[17] Her eyes lifted and focused slightly above the statue of the Virgin. Thérèse seemed immersed in joy. Her complexion became suddenly radiant with a healthy glow. Then she closed her eyes peacefully and died. It was 7:20 P.M., Thursday, September 30, 1897.

Thérèse's wake was held in the choir until the evening of Sunday, October 3. Her funeral Mass was celebrated in the convent chapel and she was buried in the Lisieux cemetery the next day, Monday, October 4. What appeared to be the end of her short, seemingly uneventful life was really just the beginning.

CHAPTER SIXTEEN

Just the Beginning

On March 7, 1898, Bishop Hugonin gave his permission for Thérèse's *Story of a Soul* to be published. Beginning in 1899 pilgrims began to flock to her grave to pray. Thérèse's cause for sainthood was presented to Rome by the Carmelites on July 9, 1906. Letters about favors received through her intercession poured into the Carmel of Lisieux. In 1910 alone, the nuns received 9,741 such letters from France and beyond. Devotion to Thérèse continued to spread. On August 14, 1921, Pope Benedict XV officially began the investigation into the sanctity of her life. At the ceremony, the pope delivered a moving homily on the importance of Thérèse's way of spiritual childhood.

On April 29, 1923, Pope Pius XI declared Thérèse "Blessed," calling her "the star of his pontificate." He canonized her on May 17, 1925. On December 14, 1927, Pope Pius XI named Saint Thérèse patron of the missions, along with Saint Francis Xavier.

On Mission Sunday, October 19, 1997, Pope John Paul II proclaimed Thérèse a doctor of the Church. She is the youngest person to have received this honor and only the third woman to join the ranks of the doctors, following after Saint Catherine of Siena and Saint Teresa of Avila.

If Thérèse's life could be summed up in one word it would have to be *love*. Thérèse love sprang from an unshakable confidence in the goodness and mercy of God; her love penetrated beyond all boundaries—even those of death. Thérèse has promised, "If God answers my desires, my heaven will be spent on earth until the end of the world. Yes, I want to spend my heaven in doing good on earth."[1] Thérèse continues to love.

. . . .

Prayer in Honor of Saint Thérèse

My Novena Rose Prayer

O little Thérèse of the Child Jesus,
please pick for me a rose
from the heavenly gardens and
send it to me as a message of love.
O Little Flower of Jesus,
ask God today to grant the favors I now place
with confidence in your hands . . . *(mention specific request)*.
Saint Thérèse, help me to always believe as you did,
in God's great love for me,
so that I might imitate your "little way" each day. Amen.

· · · · · · · · · · · ·

Reflection Questions

1. Much of Thérèse's path to holiness was lived in the midst of her family. Who have been the persons who have helped form and support my own life of faith? How can I practice Thérèse's "little way" in my daily life, among those with whom I live and work?

2. Thérèse was undeterred in trying to follow God's will as she understood it in her life. In what moments in my life have I felt the call of God? How have I responded?

3. Thérèse found many images for God's action in her life in everyday things: children's toys, flowers, etc. Do I have a favorite image of God? Is there some element in nature that reminds me of God's love and presence in my life?

4. Thérèse was convinced of the loving care of God even amid great personal suffering. How have I experienced the power of faith in my own moments of suffering?

Chronology

January 2, 1873—Thérèse was born in Alençon to Louis and Zelie Martin.

January 4, 1873—Thérèse was baptized at the church of Notre-Dame.

August 28, 1877—Zelie Martin, Thérèse's mother, dies.

November 16, 1877—The Martin family moves to *Les Buissonnets* in Lisieux.

October 2, 1882—Pauline (later known as Sister Agnes of Jesus) enters the Carmel in Lisieux.

May 8, 1884—Thérèse makes her first Communion.

October 7, 1886—Léonie enters the Poor Clares at Alençon, returning home again in December.

October 15, 1886—Marie (later known as Sister Marie of the Sacred Heart) enters the Carmel in Lisieux.

July 16, 1887—Léonie enters the Visitation convent in Caen, returning home again after several months.

November 20, 1887—Thérèse has an audience with Pope Leo XIII and asks permission to enter Carmel.

April 9, 1888—Thérèse enters the Carmel in Lisieux.

January 10, 1889—Thérèse receives the habit and begins her novitiate.

September 8, 1890—Thérèse makes her profession of vows.

May 12, 1892—Louis Martin visits Carmel for the last time before his death.

June 24, 1893—Léonie again enters the Visitation convent in Caen.

July 29, 1894—Louis Martin, Thérèse's father, dies.

September 14, 1894—Céline (later known as Sister Geneviève) enters the Carmel in Lisieux.

December 1894—Mother Agnes of Jesus (Pauline) orders Thérèse to begin writing her autobiography, later known as *Story of a Soul*.

July 20, 1895—Léonie leaves the Visitation convent; she enters for the third time in 1899 and remains, eventually becoming known as Sister Françoise-Thérèse.

April 2–3, 1896—Thérèse manifests the first serious symptoms of her illness.

April 1897—Thérèse becomes seriously ill.

July 30, 1897—Thérèse is given the Anointing of the Sick.

August 19, 1897—Thérèse receives Communion for the last time.

September 30, 1897—Thérèse dies around 7:20 P.M.

. . . .

Notes

Foreword

1. LT 74 From Thérèse to Agnes of Jesus, January 6, 1889. http://www.archives-carmel-lisieux.fr/english/carmel/index.php/lt-71-a-80/1038-lt-74-a-soeur-agnes-de-jesus © Washington Province of Discalced Carmelite Friars, Inc (ICS).

2. Thérèse of Lisieux, *Story of a Soul*, 3rd Edition, trans. by John Clarke, O.C.D. (Washington, D.C., 1996), 187. Hereinafter cited as *Story*.

3. LT 43 From Thérèse to Agnes of Jesus, March 18(?), 1888. http://www.archives-carmel-lisieux.fr/english/carmel/index.php/lt-41-a-50/932-lt-43-a-soeur-agnes-de-jesus.

4. Ibid.

5. *Story*, 194.

6. Ibid, 263.

Preface

1. *Story*, 181.

Chapter One

1. *Story*, 6.
2. Ibid.
3. Ibid., 16.
4. Ibid., 22.
5. Ibid., 23.
6. Ibid., 26.
7. Ibid.
8. Ibid., 27
9. Ibid.
10. Ibid.
11. Ibid. [no. 8], 19.
12. Ibid.
13. Ibid., 6.

Chapter Two

1. *Story*, 21.
2. Ibid., 34.
3. Ibid.
4. Ibid., 35.
5. Ibid.
6. Ibid., 36.
7. Ibid., 43.
8. Ibid., 36.
9. Ibid., 37.
10. Ibid.
11. Ibid., 38.
12. Ibid., 40.
13. Ibid., 41.

Chapter Three

1. *Story*, 45.
2. Ibid., 71.
3. Ibid., 53.
4. Ibid.
5. Ibid., 58.
6. Ibid.
7. Ibid., 65.

Chapter Four

1. *Story*, 73.
2. Ibid., 79.
3. Ibid., 80.
4. Ibid., 81.

Chapter Five

1. *Story*, 97.
2. Ibid.
3. Ibid., 98.
4. Ibid.

Chapter Six

1. *Story*, 101.
2. Ibid.
3. Ibid.
4. Ibid., 102.
5. Ibid., 103.
6. Ibid.
7. Ibid., 107.

Chapter Seven

1. *Story*, 109.
2. Ibid.
3. Ibid., 110.
4. Ibid., 111.
5. Ibid., 115.
6. Ibid., 116.
7. Ibid., 118.

Chapter Eight

1. *Story*, 123.
2. Ibid.
3. Ibid., 124.
4. Ibid., 126.
5. Ibid. [no. 141], 128.
6. Ibid., 131.
7. Ibid.
8. Ibid., 134.
9. Ibid., 134–135.
10. Ibid., 135.

Chapter Nine

1. *Story*, 143–144.

Chapter Ten

1. *Story*, 148.
2. Ibid., 149.
3. Ibid., 62.
4. Ibid., 149–150.

5. Ibid. [no. 170], 150.

6. Ibid.

Chapter Eleven

1. *Story*, 282.

2. Ibid., 159.

3. Ibid., 125.

4. Ibid., 275.

Chapter Twelve

1. *Story*, 174.

2. Ibid., 169.

3. Ibid., 171.

4. Ibid., 172.

5. See *Story*, 177–178.

6. Ibid., 178.

7. Ibid., 180.

Chapter Thirteen

1. *Story*, 239.

2. Ibid., 241.

Chapter Fourteen

1. Thérèse of Lisieux, *The Poetry of Saint Thérèse of Lisieux*, trans. by Donald Kinney, O.C.D. (Washington, D.C., 1996), 90.

2. *Story*, 194.

Chapter Fifteen

1. *Story*, 245.

2. Ibid., 258.

3. Ibid., 259.

4. Ibid., 262.

5. Thérèse of Lisieux, *St. Thérèse of Lisieux: Her Last Conversations*, trans. by John Clarke, O.C.D. (Washington D.C., 1977), 143.

6. *Story*, 263.

7. *Conversations*, 102.

8. Ibid., 123–124.

9. *Conversations*, 163.

10. Ibid.

11. *Story*, 188.

12. *Conversations*, 91.

13. Ibid., 200–201.

14. *Story*, 268.

15. *Conversations*, 202.

16. *Story*, 270.

17. *Conversations*, 246.

Chapter Sixteen

1. *Conversations*, 102.

BOOKS & MEDIA

A mission of the Daughters of St. Paul

As apostles of Jesus Christ, evangelizing today's world:

We are CALLED to holiness
by God's living Word and Eucharist.

We COMMUNICATE the Gospel message
through our lives and through all
available forms of media.

We SERVE the Church
by responding to the hopes and needs
of all people with the Word of God,
in the spirit of St. Paul.

For more information visit our Web site:
www.pauline.org.

BOOKS & MEDIA

The Daughters of St. Paul operate book and media centers at the following addresses. Visit, call, or write the one nearest you today, or find us at www.pauline.org.

CALIFORNIA
3908 Sepulveda Blvd, Culver City, CA 90230	310-397-8676
935 Brewster Avenue, Redwood City, CA 94063	650-369-4230
5945 Balboa Avenue, San Diego, CA 92111	858-565-9181

FLORIDA
145 S.W. 107th Avenue, Miami, FL 33174	305-559-6715

HAWAII
1143 Bishop Street, Honolulu, HI 96813	808-521-2731

ILLINOIS
172 North Michigan Avenue, Chicago, IL 60601	312-346-4228

LOUISIANA
4403 Veterans Memorial Blvd, Metairie, LA 70006	504-887-7631

MASSACHUSETTS
885 Providence Hwy, Dedham, MA 02026	781-326-5385

MISSOURI
9804 Watson Road, St. Louis, MO 63126	314-965-3512

NEW YORK
64 W. 38th Street, New York, NY 10018	212-754-1110

SOUTH CAROLINA
243 King Street, Charleston, SC 29401	843-577-0175

TEXAS

Currently no book center; for parish exhibits or outreach evangelization, contact: 210–488–4123 or SanAntonio@paulinemedia.com

VIRGINIA
1025 King Street, Alexandria, VA 22314	703-549-3806

CANADA
3022 Dufferin Street, Toronto, ON M6B 3T5	416-781-9131